# THE WICKED AND THE QUICK

*Memories of a Seventies Biker: The second year*

S. P. Muir

The Wicked and the Quick – memories of a 70's biker: the second year © 2025 by S. P. Muir. All Rights Reserved.

All rights reserved. No part of this book may be reproduced in any form or by any electronic or mechanical means including information storage and retrieval systems, without permission in writing from the author. The only exception is by a reviewer, who may quote short excerpts in a review.

Cover designed by S. P. Muir

S. P. Muir
Visit my website at www.spmuir.com

ISBN-9798313097787

# Motorcycle books by S. P. Muir

1 – You're Where Now?
*Memoirs of a Despatch Rider*

2 – Back This Way
*Memoirs of a Despatch Rider volume two*

3 – Call Me Empty
*Memoirs of a Despatch Rider volume three*

4 – Sixteener special
*Memories of a 70's Biker: the first year*

5 – The Wicked and the Quick
*Memories of a 70's Biker: the second year*

# CONTENTS

1: Pride Goes Before a Fall ................................................................1
2: the road goes ever on ................................................................15
3: outings and wheelies ................................................................30
4: broken bones................................................................................37
5: pubs and punctures ...................................................................44
6: frustration and odd decisions...................................................49
7: slow and steady ..........................................................................63
8: christmas, snow, and ice............................................................68
9: heartbreak and a fall from grace ..............................................74
10: the quickest of the quick .........................................................81
11: silver jubilee ..............................................................................94
12: surprises good and bad..........................................................103
13: delight and disaster ................................................................112
14: surgery and a new beginning ...............................................124
15: a terrifying conversation .......................................................141
16: why so quick?..........................................................................153

S. P. Muir

*Dedicated to all the bikers out there, old or young.*

# 1: PRIDE GOES BEFORE A FALL

Anticipation is bitter-sweet. For many, many weeks now I'd been dreaming about reaching the ripe old age of seventeen. The age at which I could hit the road on a real bike. And that day had finally arrived. My poor faithful Fizzy was stashed away at the back of the garage and I was now one of the elite; I had a big bike, a proper bike. I tried really hard to look casual as I put my jacket on and grabbed my crash helmet. But there was no disguising the fact that I was almost fainting with anticipation of what was to come. I walked out the front door and paused to admire the glistening RD250B that was now my bike to ride. Then...

To be honest, I can't remember exactly how it happened. The next thing I remember, I was happily bundling through my estate towards the Rochester Road. In reality, happily is an enormous understatement. I was floating on air with unbridled ecstasy. I was a man. One of the big boys. And my bike was the fastest, wickedest, best handling two-fifty on the market.

It was another glorious 1976 summer morning, which made the experience all the more enjoyable. I didn't open the bike up, I just glided along the Rochester Road at a satisfyingly quick 60 mph. I hadn't gone too far before I saw my old 'friend' on his Kawasaki S1C coming towards me. The stuck-up prig hadn't acknowledged me since the day he'd moved up from *his* Fizzy; but this morning – and every morning from then on – the old cheery wave was back. His sleek, blue triple flashed by leaving a smug little grin on my face. His bike may have been better looking; it may have had an extra cylinder; but my Yam could blow it into the weeds if I ever gave him a race.

The story of how I came by the RD250 is explained in the final two chapters of *Sixteener Special*, the first book in this series; so I won't go over it again. Suffice it to say that my faithful old Fizz was now stashed at the back of the garage waiting to be sold – if I could be arsed to get round to it that is. My shiny, low mileage, nine-month-old RD250B had left the lovely purple Fizz a forgotten, unloved piece of unwanted metal niggling somewhere at the back of my mind. As it turned out a friend of a friend soon came knocking on the door enquiring as to whether I still had it. And that was the end of that particular episode. The symbol of my first year on two wheels was gone, and I couldn't give a stuff. It's different now of course, but memories are what they are.

But back to the story. I arrived at the Chatham shop where I worked and stowed the RD round the back, just as I'd been doing with my Fizz for almost a year. I stood for a good five minutes just staring at the gleaming beast, still unable to quite believe it was mine. Eventually I tore myself away and went into work. Of course, the word 'work' was a bit misleading on that day. I was so anxious for five-thirty to finally arrive I was unable to concentrate on anything. Customers went unserved and eventually my manager got so frustrated with me, he sent me out the back to tidy up the stockroom. And very little tidying up got done, I can tell you. I spent the whole afternoon daydreaming about my new bike.

Eventually, knocking off time came around, and I shot out the door like a bullet from a gun. I ran round the back and pulled on my lid. Once again trembling with excitement I unlocked the bike, shoved the key into the ignition lock, and threw a leg over the mighty beast. No need for gloves in the baking heat of that glorious 1976 summer. So without a second's delay, I kicked the engine into life. Oh, the exquisite sound of a highly tuned two-stroke twin. It still sends shivers up my spine whenever I hear one. Paddling the bike backwards and around to face the exit, I finally stamped it into gear and trickled up the short alleyway and then out into the traffic.

It's no boast to say that after a year on my Fizzy – even passing my test on it – I was a pretty good rider. So filtering past all the cars clogging the road was a breeze. It's probably worth mentioning that although I had a full licence, it only entitled me to ride a moped without L-plates. I would need to retake the test on a proper bike to once again discard them and take a passenger on the back – unless *they* had a full licence of course. A rule that has now changed I believe. I was furious about the stupidity of it all. After all, the moped test and the bike test were identical – and I mean identical! So why the hell should I go through the whole rigmarole again? But that's what the law said, so I had to suffer the embarrassment of those dreaded 'ells' once again. And to add to the frustration, my girlfriend, Jo, was severely underwhelmed that after several months of riding pillion on the Fizz, she was now banned from coming on the back.

The ride home from work was wonderful. Once I'd cleared all the heavy traffic and had turned onto the Rochester Road, I gave the bike a bit of throttle. Not too much yet, just enough to cruise along at the same happy sixty. No need to rush; after the paltry forty-five I was used to cruising at, sixty felt really fast. And the knowledge of all that power I was keeping in reserve was strangely thrilling.

When I got home, I changed out of my suit and into something more sensible. I greedily wolfed down my dinner and shot back out to the bike. Since it was a Monday, I had no Jehovah's Witness meeting to attend (see Sixteener Special) so I was meant to be going over to Jo's. I'd ummed and ahed about it while scoffing my dinner. It was a bit of a dilemma. I wanted to see her, and I wanted to show her the bike, but I was also desperate to just ride it. In the end I came up with a compromise. I'd go over to her place until about eight thirty and then I'd make a quick getaway to enjoy the bike. So that's exactly what I did.

I can't describe the feeling of swinging through the country lanes to her house. I used to thrash the poor little Fizz mercilessly along them, but to fly through those bends without going much above 5,500 revs was... well, it was indescribable. I was beside myself with excitement and joy.

Jo looked the bike over approvingly. "So when are you going to put in for your test?" she asked with one of her lovely '*you'd better do what I say*' smiles.

"Not just yet," I replied with a serious look. "I think I need to get used to it first." You'll no doubt remember my amazing talent for being a lazy, procrastinating, irresponsible little sod. Okay, I'd applied for my moped test as soon as I'd read that you could, but even then I'd left it up to my stepmother, Gwen, to post the application form. And since I was so angry with the DVLA, I was by no means in a hurry at all this time. Talk about cutting off your nose etcetera.

After my pleasant, if frustrating visit with the girl I loved, I hurried away on the bike which I probably loved even more. *"I know,"* I thought. *"I'll ride around my estate for a while. I'm bound to run into one of mates; or even better some of the hallowed two-fifty riders. They're bound to give me some respect now."*

In the end it was a bit of both. As I trundled around the narrow roads, I spotted an RD250C coming towards me. It was my friend – well, at the time he was more of a friend of a friend – Smiffy. I decided to play it cool and gave him a casual wave. When we were past each other, I glanced in my mirror. To my delight he'd spun around and was screaming after me. I pulled over and almost immediately he was beside me.

"You're on the road with it then," he said just a touch admiringly.

"Yeah. Started riding it today."

"What's it go like?"

"Um... Really quick," I replied lying through my teeth. I still hadn't taken it over six grand.

"Come on, I'll race you past the Chef."

And he was away. The Little Chef was a roadside café type affair on the A2. I was a bit reluctant to play this game just yet. Nearly all the big bikes would race down the slight hill on the motorway-like A2. There was even a bridge spanning the road where you could watch whoever was racing. But I didn't want that "whoever" to be me before I'd got used to the bike. But neither could I not. I would never live such cowardice down, so I stamped the bike into gear and followed Smiffy off the estate and along the short country lane to where the race would begin.

I pulled up alongside him as he stopped at the end of the lane where the races always began. Both bikes would pull out onto the larger road then onto the curving slip road that joined the A2 itself. Then... *Blam.* Throttles would be wacked hard against the stop and the race was on.

To my dismay, Smiffy was immediately away in a smoking cloud of two-stroke. After hesitating for a fraction of a second, I followed on but just a little more carefully. I reached the slip road, heeled the bike over, and wound the throttle wide open. Suddenly, for the first time since swinging a leg over the bike, the engine hit its powerband.

Now let me cast your mind back to when I bought the bike. If you remember from *Sixteener Special* the bloke I'd bought the RD from had issued an ominous warning.

"So what bike have you got at the moment?" he'd asked seriously.

"An FS1E," I'd replied.

"Hmm," he'd murmured sagely. "Then you'd better be really careful. If you don't, when that RD hits its powerband, as sure as God made daisies it'll spit you off."

Although I was still leant over a fair way, the RD didn't quite spit me off. But I was so unprepared for the sheer violence of it (well to me anyway) I traversed all three lanes. Boy did I leave some skid marks – just not on the road. From that moment on I meekly followed Smiffy at an outrageously fast (not) seventy.

When we met up at the turnoff, Smiffy turned on me. "What the hell happened; where were you?" he asked.

I swallowed hard. How could I admit the truth? "Back wheel stepped right out as we came onto the A2," I lied. "Really thought I had a puncture."

"Looks okay to me," Smiffy said doubtfully.

"Yeah; must have been a patch of oil or something," I said lamely.

"Yeah, must have been. You wanna go again?"

Frantically I tried to think of a reason to decline the offer. Eventually all I could think of was, "Nah, I gottta get home and help my dad with something."

Smiffy nodded. "Okay; maybe another time then."

Was it me or was there a note of scepticism in Smiffy's voice? "Yeah, another time."

With another sharp nod Smiffy stamped his bike into gear and screamed away. I was to learn that Smiffy's style of riding was balls out all the time. I'm not sure he realised that there were more than two positions on the throttle. Good job he was probably the most skillful rider I've ever met.

By now it was beginning to get dark, so I headed back to the estate. The route I chose took me past the car park for the recreation centre on Thong Lane. There was often a gathering there, and today I spotted a couple of bikes with what looked like several girls grouped around them. Brilliant! A chance to show off without screwing up.

I swung into the car park and as casually as I could, I pulled up beside another RD250B. There was also an older model RD250 there, but I didn't recognise the bloke sitting on it. He looked two or three years older than me – about my sister's age – and was obviously a right hard nut. I knew a couple of the half dozen or so girls there though. Snooty cows who'd been in my year at school. They were the popular girls and were friends with my sister. They'd always treated me with either disgust or disdain, but my heart swelled with pride at the way they looked at me today. They all had such admiring looks on their faces; oh what a babe magnet this bike was.

The owner of the 250B was standing with them and was giving my bike an approving look. He was someone I'd seen around once or twice, but I didn't really know him.

"Nice bike," he said coolly.

"Yeah. I only started riding it today. Bloody relief to get off my Fizzy."

"You had a Fizz?" the hard nut said getting off his bike.

"Yeah. One of the purple ones."

"You wasn't one of the gang of peds that tried chasing me down a few weeks back was you?" He asked the question with a big disarming grin on his hard-as-nails face.

"Probably," I replied returning his grin. Obviously, I didn't have a clue what he was on about, but I was trying to impress the girls.

"Have you opened it up yet?" the 250B owner asked in a friendly, conversational voice.

I was just about to take my lid off to answer him when *BAM!* An express train crashed into the side of my head. I was sent sprawling to the ground with my bike on top of me.

"Take your f***ing lid off," the hard nut demanded angrily. "I'm gonna beat your face into a bloody pulp."

I tried to crawl out from under the bike, but my head was spinning from the effect of his fist. I couldn't understand how he hadn't broken every bone in his hand.

"Why?" I managed to whimper pathetically.

"Cos you tried chasing me down. Well you've caught me now so take your lid off and stand up."

"It wasn't me," I cried in a thin quavering voice as I tried to get my legs free from the bike. Thankfully, the 250B rider helped by picking the bike up and putting it on its side stand.

"You just said it was."

"I was lying!" It was a good job it was well past dusk and I still had my lid on, otherwise everyone would have seen my tears.

"You're f***ing lying now."

"I'm not," I wailed helplessly. "Honestly, I just wanted to sound hard."

At that moment the 250B rider put a friendly hand on my shoulder. "Look mate," he said softly. "If I was you I'd just get on your bike and f**k off quick."

I needed no more encouragement. In a flash I was back on the bike, and after about five kicks, it burst indignantly into life. I caught a glance at the girls' faces in my headlight. Their expressions were a mixture of pity and scorn. It's a sight that still haunts me to this day.

As I headed home, I felt such shame as I'd never felt before. And my bike seemed to share my feelings. For some odd reason it now refused to tick over. I would have to take a look at it first thing in the morning.

As I lay in bed that night, something odd happened to me. The self-pity and shame began to morph into something I'd never known before. Something had changed inside me, and with a steely resolve, I swore never to back down from a fight again – no matter what the odds. And it's a vow that I've kept to this very day.

The next morning, I went out to the bike a little earlier than usual. It didn't take long to identify the problem with the bike. The left hand tickover screw was missing. It must have dropped out when the bike had fallen on top of me, but I couldn't understand how. Still, it took me just a few minutes to fix it. At the back of the garage was a tin of screws and to my relief, one of them was the right size and thread. Okay it wasn't tapered and there was no spring to hold it in place, but as a temporary fix, it worked perfectly. And that's how it stayed until the following Sunday.

I'd been a good boy and had gone to the Kingdom Hall for the morning meeting. After dinner I went out for another ride. As I rode past the pub where all the bikers would gather, I spotted three blokes standing near their bikes in the car park having a good old chinwag. I recognised them straight away. There was my good friend Ivor with his blue Yamaha YB100, Smiffy with his 250C, and... The third guy was the bloke from the other night who'd kindly lifted the bike off me. I couldn't face the embarrassment of joining them with *him* there, so I decided to ride on by. Ivor, however, had other ideas. He waved frantically and gestured for me to join them. Reluctantly, I did as I was told.

"Alright Muir?" Ivor said enthusiastically. "You're on the road then."

I thought it was a stupid statement since I'd been on the road for over a year, but I let it slide. "Yeah. I started riding it on Monday."

"I know," Smiffy said. "You taken it past the Chef yet?" he asked with a wicked little grin. I was certain he'd guessed that I'd bottled it.

I was suddenly aware that the bloke from the other night looked acutely embarrassed. He smiled sheepishly and fished something out of his pocket. "Here," he said handing it to me. "This is yours. I took it the other night, but if I'd known you was a mate of Smiffy's I wouldn't have taken it."

I looked at the object and blinked in surprise. It was the missing tickover screw.

"That's right," Smiffy said in a curiously flat voice. "Tony didn't realize you that were one of us."

After chatting for about half an hour I left them and headed over to Jo's. All the way there Smiffy's words reverberated around my head. "Tony didn't realize you were one of us." *One of us!* For the first time in my life, I felt a sense of belonging. I should have felt that with the Jehovah's Witnesses, but somehow I never did quite fit in. So as the months went by, I spent more time with 'The Boat Mob' as they – we – were known. I even started skipping a few JW meetings; something that gradually became more frequent as time rolled by.

At last, there was somewhere I could belong.

# 2: THE ROAD GOES EVER ON

It was late august and by now I had really got to grips with my wicked bronze beast. And rather than something to be wary of, the power band was something I now revelled in. I just couldn't get enough of the sudden rush of power that exploded in at around six grand. Oh, my bike was just so *wicked!* To add to my joy, I had a week's holiday booked – from work that is, not an *actual* holiday. Times were a little different back then. So what to do with my seven days of free time? Jo was at work as were all the Boat Mob. Only my JW friends, Mark and Martin, didn't have full-time jobs. They were what's called Pioneers. Their task was to clock up seventy or so hours a month knocking on doors to sell the Watchtower and Awake magazines. I'm sure you've all had that knock on the door yourselves at some point. All Jehovah's Witnesses are expected to put in some time 'on the work' as it's called. If they don't do enough hours, they are considered spiritually weak and can expect a bit of a 'talking to'. I must admit, I did all I could to get out of it and received a few scolding chats myself.

My JW mother had been expecting me to go and live with her as soon as I'd left school (the story behind that idea is a long and painful one) but she soon realised that this wasn't going to happen. So disgusted was she that she decided to become a 'Special Pioneer' which meant she would be sent to live anywhere in the country 'where the need is greatest'. In other words, where there wasn't enough door knocking going on. So in late July of '76, she found herself living in Tewksbury, Gloucestershire. A lovely little Town, so I was told. As my holiday drew ever closer, a plan began to formulate in my tiny little brain. Perhaps my Witness friends Martin or Mark fancied coming with me on a run out to visit my mum.

I pondered about which of the two to ask. True, I'd started getting on with Mark better than Martin, but he only had a CD175, whereas Martin had that sweet, remarkably quick, gold coloured CB250K4. So I made the decision to broach the idea with Martin. To my surprise and delight he was all up for it. So after a quick phone call to my mum, it was all set. My first road trip was all planned. Martin could only manage four days, but that didn't matter a bit. It was still an adventure, the idea of which was making my head spin with excitement.

Luggage was something I hadn't really thought about. I only needed to take a couple of changes of clothing along with my toothbrush, but it was still something that had me flummoxed.

"Just put it in a carrier bag and bungee it to your back seat," Martin scoffed rather derisively. I really liked Martin but he could be a right arrogant sod at times. And anyway, I didn't possess any bungee cords. Fortunately, Martin had a couple he could spare. What do you mean, I could have bought some? I was as tight as a duck's arse and anyway, I wanted all my money to spend on our little holiday.

At last the day arrived. At nine o'clock in the morning I rolled up at Martin's with both the oil and fuel tanks full to the brim, and my luggage securely strapped to the back seat. The pair of us had plotted the route on a map the previous day, and I was itching to get going. Martin, however, was giving his bike a final check before lift-off.

I hovered impatiently over him which clearly annoyed him because he gave me a curt, "You should check your bike too. I doubt you've already thought of it."

He was right; I hadn't. With a shamed face I checked the chain and tyre pressures. I knew the chain would be okay; I'd suffered a disaster from maintenance neglect on my Fizzy when I'd first got it, so my chain had been meticulously maintained ever since. My tyre pressures were a different matter, however. That was quickly rectified with some vigorous exercise on a foot pump. The sound of air going into the tyres was accompanied by a fair amount of tutting from my haughty travel companion.

Then at last, we were off. Keeping to tradition, since Martin's trusty Honda was slower than my Yam he took the lead. The grin on my face threatened to split my face open as we wended our way through the estate and then out onto the A2 'motorway'. I settled into my seat and just let the road flow past at the seventy mph pace Martin was setting.

Now since I'm pretty sure you've read *Sixteener Special*, you'll probably remember the riding position I'd adopted way on back when I'd first got my Fizz. I'd been pathetic for the first few days – in fact I'm not quite sure how I'd survived. My mastery of the clutch was so bad that my pull away technique was to paddle the bike forward with my feet and feed (or dump) the clutch in once I was moving. I looked a right prat in another way too. Like many novice riders I've seen over the years, I was sitting so far back I was practically on the back seat. Fortunately, I was spotted by a guy called Nigel who was a friend of Martin's.

To me, Nigel was something of a hero. I didn't know him that well but since he had a Suzuki T500, in my mind he was a god. And the way he sat on that big blue stroker was something to see. So, with some help and advice from him, I soon mastered the clutch and was emulating his riding position perfectly. It probably looked a bit silly on a moped, but on my RD it made me look as wicked as the bike.

For some reason, the RD250B was graced with rather high and wide bars. Much higher than Smiffy's C version. They clearly weren't that practical for an out and out sports bike, but boy did they look good tipped forward. And by sitting right where the seat met the tank – practically *on* the tank – it gave the rider a fantastically hunched and aggressive stance. As I say, wicked.

So the morning of our adventure I sat behind my friend and smugly grinned to myself. With the K4's flat bars, Martin could only sit one way – boring. Whereas I was clearly king of the road. I didn't feel quite so smug as the long miles rolled by though. I just knew Martin wasn't as uncomfortable as I was.

We finally made it into London and that's where we encountered our first problem. Neither of us knew the capital that well, although Martin had more idea of where we were going than I did. After a couple of wrong turns, we made it right across town to where we could pick up the A40. And that's when things really went pear shaped. We suddenly realised we had entered the slip road for the M40 motorway – a *real* motorway. Obviously, I wasn't allowed on it with my L plates, so we stopped where we were and had an earnest discussion.

"I think we'll have to try and push the bikes back off the slip road," Martin said thoughtfully.

"But that's going to be really dangerous," I replied, anxiously eyeing the traffic speeding past us. "Why don't we just take my L plates off and carry on. We can come off at the next exit."

Martin blew out his cheeks thoughtfully. "I don't think we should," he said seriously. "It's illegal. I definitely think it would be better to just push the bikes back."

I knew what he was thinking. Jehovah's Witnesses are supposed to obey all the laws of the land without breaking any. In my experience though, that rule can get a bit fuzzy at times; especially when it comes to speed limits.

"But pushing the bikes back's illegal too," I replied getting irritated by his nonsense. "And it's more dangerous. And anyway, I have actually got a full licence, so it's only half breaking the law if we carry on."

"A moped licence doesn't count.," he said scornfully. "They're not allowed on motorways either."

"But surely…"

"No," Martin said firmly. "We'll push them back off the slip road. At least then we're trying to correct our mistake rather than carrying on with it."

And so with much bitter muttering from me, that's exactly what we did. Now the entrance to the M40 slip road is (or was) a tight, narrow blind bend with a high wall on either side. Three times we were almost hit by cars coming around that bend. Thankfully, we didn't encounter a lorry or we'd have been toast. I still believe we should have followed my plan and just ripped off my stupid L plates. But since Martin was several years older than me, I didn't have the balls to insist. Still, it was soon over, and we were back in London traffic and back on track.

I was pretty miffed about the incident but once we were out onto the A40 proper, I began to relax. The sun was beating down, the breeze was keeping me cool. We were also now travelling at a more sedate sixty to sixty-five, which was taking some of the pressure off my shoulders. And the scenery was fantastic. Never in my life had I felt such freedom.

Although we were travelling at a pretty sedate rate of knots, every now and then we came upon a slow-moving car or lorry. Martin would close in and then at just the right moment he'd crack the throttle open and off he'd go accompanied by the Honda's high-pitched roar. I'd then wait for my turn. Wait for it, wait for it.... Then stamp down two gears and nail the throttle to the stop. Then my wonderful, powerful, *wicked* RD would scream past the offending obstacle making Martin's Honda look like the slug it actually wasn't. Yes, my RD250B was just *WICKED!*

I had no way of knowing how short my relationship with this wicked, evil little beast would be though.

Eventually, the heady excitement of the long ride (tempered slightly by the aches inflicted on my scrawny body by the high bars and severe riding position) came to an end. We'd arrived. Tewksbury was a lovely quaint little town, and it didn't take long for me and my travelling buddy to locate the house where we were billeted. My mum lived in a little caravan with no room for us two blokes, so she'd arranged for us to stay with someone from her congregation. For some reason that I can't remember, the nice couple we stayed with had a spare bedroom equipped with bunk beds. So that's where we slept. Our bikes were safely stashed in the back garden each night.

I don't remember much about our time in Tewksbury, although I do remember a few coffees or meals in the local cafes. I also remember the guilt trips my mum laid on me for not having gone to live with her – she was an expert at that sort of thing. Even so, it was a very nice few days. Despite not remembering very much about our stay though, there is one specific day that stands out. And I remember that day perfectly.

It was Martin's idea. We were in our bedroom preparing to settle down for the night when it came to him. He was studying a map of the area when he suddenly sat bolt upright.

"Hey look at this," he said pointing at the map. "They've named a town after me."

"Where?" I asked, coming over to get a look.

"There, see; Stroud."

"Oh yeah. Hey you're family's famous."

"I tell you what, shall we take a ride over there tomorrow?"

I grinned. "Sure, looks like it should be a nice day out."

So next morning we set out on what would be one of the best rides of my life. Martin had picked the perfect route. It was all country lanes with a couple of stretches on A roads. I've tried many times over the years to trace that route on a map. But since at the time

I hadn't bothered to take any notice, I can't say for sure exactly where we went. I just followed Martin and enjoyed the ride – and what a ride it was.

We didn't particularly rush, we just kind of 'hustled'. My RD seemed to be revelling in it. We swung through the wide sweeping bends with hardly any need to slow down; just a little dab here and there on the back brake to steady the ship. Even Martin's CB250 seemed to be having a good time. And the view! To our right was a huge drop with what seemed like the whole of Gloucestershire visible to the eye. We couldn't resist the opportunity to stop and marvel at the fantastic vista.

We found a nice little pull-in to stop at and wandered the few yards to the cliff-like drop. We didn't go right up to the edge since the ground sloped towards the cliff and got steadily steeper as it went. There were a fair few bushes and such, but almost nothing in the way to spoil the view. We took our lids off and stood there marvelling at the wonder of it all.

"Fantastic, isn't it?" Martin said in a hushed voice.

"It sure is," I replied casually swinging my helmet by its still fastened strap. It was one of those D ring fasteners that I came to love. No need to completely undo it. Just loosen it enough to slip it over my chin. It was something that really came in handy a few years down the line when I became a despatch rider.

"I tell you what, it was worth coming just to see this," Martin said with a smile.

"I know. I mean look at it all," I replied, waving towards the view with the hand holding my crash hat. I'm not sure why I used that hand, but it turned out to be a bad idea. For the first and last time in my life, that D ring fastener let go. My lid hit the ground and started rolling towards the edge.

"NO!" I cried desperately as it bounced towards its doom. I started to run to save it but then pulled up sharply almost slipping on the steeply sloping grass. My heart sank as my helmet bounced over the edge into its fatal drop. Except it didn't fall to its death. Just over the edge a scraggy little bush was bravely clinging to the side of the cliff, and my lid rolled into its life-saving clutches.

"What the..." Martin said with a touch of anger in his voice. "How the hell did you manage to do something that stupid?!" He wasn't the most forgiving person I'd ever met.

"It just slipped," I replied somewhat pathetically. "What am I going to do now? It's right on the edge."

"You'll have to go and get it. You can't ride on without it."

*"But it's right on the edge!"* I repeated desperately.

Martin shrugged. "Well I'm not going to get it."

I looked to where my lid lay nestled in the straggly branches. There was no way I could simply walk over and reclaim it; not with the slope that grew so much steeper towards the edge. I swallowed hard and did the only thing I could do. I dropped to my hands and knees and crawled. By the time I reached the cliff edge I was on my belly. I must confess, I have a very healthy fear of heights. Not the fear of falling, you understand; just a pragmatic realisation of what happens when that fall comes to an abrupt end. I'm fine on ladders and stuff, but cliffs? No thank you. I truly believe that rock climbers are insane. And yet here I was reaching out into the void; at least that's how it seemed. And my helmet wasn't exactly easy to grab. It was facing the wrong way meaning I had to reach right over the edge. That might be a slight exaggeration, but that was exactly how it felt. My heart was pounding in my chest while my breathing was reduced to quick, short, desperate gasps. If I fumbled it, my precious full-face lid would be gone forever – or worse, so could I!

Eventually, I managed to get my fingers over the chin piece. I held my breath as I gingerly eased it round so I could get a better grip. Success! It was soon safely back on solid ground. Almost sobbing with relief, I crawled back towards the bikes.

"Nicely done," Martin said with genuine admiration in his voice. Then, "Maybe we should get back on the road and push on."

Swallowing hard I nodded.

Without further ado I pulled my wayward lid on and did up the strap. How the hell it had broken free I'll never know. I climbed onto the RD and kicked it back into life. Martin did the same – well at least he pressed the starter button, or 'pansy kicker' as electric starters became known amongst the Boat Mob. He glanced over his shoulder to see if I was ready. I gave a quick nod and we were away.

It didn't take long for me to calm down again. That exciting two stroke exhaust noise accompanied by the early RD250 intake moan soothed my nerves no end. After swinging through the bends for another couple of miles we arrived at our destination: Stroud.

To be honest, the town was a bit of an anti-climax. We wandered around for a while but soon got bored with it. I'm not sure what we expected, and the lure of the bikes soon had us riding back the way we'd come. This time, however, we didn't stop to admire the view.

\* \* \*

As I've said, I don't remember much about our stay with my mum but I do know it was enjoyable, even if it wasn't exactly memorable. However, there was an incident that did stand out, and one that was to become rather significant in the next couple of months.

It couldn't last. The great heatwave had to end, and typical of my luck, it ended during that nice little holiday in Gloucestershire. Martin and I were invited to dinner with one of the Elders in mum's congregation. It was a pleasant evening – especially for Martin. He really was a full-on Jehovah's Witness, and the conversation was very much about the Bible and stuff. I enjoyed it as well but couldn't really add much to what was said. At about ten o'clock we said our goodbyes and headed off back to where we were staying. We'd only gone about a hundred yards when the heavens opened. Within what seemed like seconds, I was soaked. And so was the bike. It was the first time the RD had seen rain since I'd got it, and boy did it rain.

And that's when I found out another reason why the bloke had sold it so cheap. After about half a mile it dropped onto one pot. What a nightmare of a journey that ride became. I was cold, soaked, I could hardly see, and my now impotent bike sounded like a wet fart. Good job we only had a couple of miles to go.

I was broken hearted when we got back. My precious RD250 was sick. What the hell was I going to do? We were heading off for home the next morning, and there was no way the bike could do a hundred or so miles on one cylinder. Luckily, our host had a can of WD40 in his garage. We gave the plug caps a good coating and squirted some up under the tank towards the coils. To my relief, the next morning the magic spray had done its job, and we were away.

The journey home was pretty much a repeat of the one before – minus the awkward bit concerning trying to get onto the M40! And that was it. The end of a marvellous adventure. But as for the one-cylinder incident, it wasn't the last time rain was to cause the same problem. And WD40 was to prove less and less effective every time. My love for the RD waned almost every time it rained, and I became more and more frustrated with the damned thing.

# 3: OUTINGS AND WHEELIES

Being a Jehovah's Witness wasn't all meetings and door knocking. There was actually a fair bit of socialising going on with us youngsters. I'd met Jo at one of the many parties and there was a bit of football in a park during the summer. There were also a few trips to Streatham skating rink. I'd been on a couple of these trips on my moped, but two or three weeks after getting back from Gloucestershire another visit to the skating rink was planned.

So one evening when there wasn't a JW meeting or study or whatever else the controlling Organisation inflicted on everyone, the game was on. I can't remember where we all met up – it might well have been at Martin's house – but I do remember that there were quite a few of us. Jo was a bit miffed that she had to go in a car rather than on the back of my RD, but even so, everyone was looking forward to a good time. And indeed, a good time was had by all. I'd like to boast about my amazing skill on the ice but since I moved around on it about as competently as a blind and drunken camel, I'll just leave that bit out of the narrative. It was nice to be out and about with Jo though, even if cuddles were out of the question in such oh-so-strict company.

Once it was over and everyone was changing back into their normal footwear, I hurried to be the first changed and slipped outside to where the bike sat in the car park. I was just going to sit on it until the others came out, but I just couldn't resist it. That RD250 was just so *wicked*. I fired it up and pulled out into the road.

Now the car park was behind the building with the entrance on the left and the exit on the right. So after pulling out into the traffic, I did a kind of circuit. Out of the exit then back into the entrance. Lovely. But then the bike's wickedness possessed my mind. It was infected by that wonderful engine's exhaust note. Oh yes, it was all too easy. On my third outing, I gave it some revs, popped the clutch and.... Wheeeee. A perfect wheelie. I dropped the front down wheel just in time to pull back into the car park. "Again," the bike seemed to cry. So I did. And again, and again.

It's really odd, but for some reason the old bill don't take too kindly to little oiks pulling big wheelies outside skating rinks. I was honestly surprised when a police car pulled into the car park behind me and flashed their blue lights.

"Oh crap," I thought to myself. "I bet I'm in for a good talking to here." And boy was I. I took off my gloves, slipped off my lid and plonked it on one of the mirrors. I then waited for the two angry boys in blue to approach me.

"What the bloody hell do you think you're doing?" one of them shouted.

I decided to play dumb. I gave them my best imitation of total confusion, and in a pathetic, quavering voice said, "I...I don't know what you mean."

"Don't take the piss," the other copper growled. "You know exactly what we're talking about." Oh, such language from our brave upholders of the law.

"I'm sorry but I don't," I replied almost in tears that weren't *altogether* fake. "I..."

"Doing flaming a wheelie on the public highway!" the first one explained sharply. "You realise such behaviour could lose you your license for dangerous driving."

"Oh, that," I said trying to look abashed. "Erm..."

"Yes that." Snapped the second policeman.

With my brain flying at warp speed, I came up with an answer that kept me in good stead may times after this awful awakening. "To be honest," I said looking pleadingly from one to the other. "I've only just got the bike. I had a little moped before and this thing is just so much more powerful. I'm afraid I gave it a little too much throttle and the front wheel just came up. It scared me so I pulled in here to calm down." I prayed they hadn't seen me going round and round. That would have scuppered my whole defence. I glanced around to see if my friends were coming out yet. Again, that would have blown my hurriedly made up excuse.

"Humph," they both snorted in stereo. "Well you're just going to have to be more careful in future."

"Yeah, we've got your registration number, and we'll alert the whole force. If anyone catches you doing anything stupid again, we'll throw the book at you."

That was bullshit of course but I decided to play along. "Of course, thank you," I said throwing as much gratitude into my voice as I could. "I'll be really careful from now on. And I'm sure I'll get the hang of the bike soon."

"You'd better. Now off you go, and remember, we're watching you." With that they sauntered back to their car without so much as a backward glance. I fumbled with my crash hat, taking as long as I could to put it on. *Please go,* I begged silently. Thankfully, they started the car up straight away and glided past. They were gone just in time. As soon as their taillights disappeared into the traffic, my friends came flooding out of the exit. Jo hurried over to me with *that* look on her face.

"You shot out pretty quick," she said suspiciously. "Why?"

"I just wanted to get out to the bike. You know how it is."

"Hmmm. Sometimes I think you love that thing more than you love me."

"Never! I love you more than anything thing in the world." I would have reinforced the sentiment with a kiss, but with a couple of the more zealous Jehovah's Witness friends watching us closely – especially Martin – it was out of the question. I found out sometime later that Martin fancied his chances with Jo himself and was just a tiny bit jealous that we were a secret item. I was really getting pissed off with all the strict rules about not being a couple unless you were planning marriage. *What?* I hear you ask. *Marriage?* Oh yes. The reason being that the pair involved might get carried away and commit the sin of fornication. That's having sex out of wedlock to those of a secular mind-set. If only they knew that *that* particular horse had bolted a couple of weeks ago. Whoops.

"You'd better," she said thawing a little.

"Come on Jo," someone called from one of the cars.

"See you tomorrow?" she asked in that, you *will* see me tomorrow voice.

"Of course. I'll come over straight after work."

She gave me that smile that made my heart do somersaults then hurried over to the car. I blew out a breath of relief and wondered how long it would be before I had the courage to tell her about my little brush with the law. She could get really miffed about such things. But then again, at other times she could laugh about them. I shook my head. I did love her, but boy she could be hard work at times. I remembered the latter days of my Fizzy ownership when I could take her on the back. The freedom we'd had to erm... go for a ride as it were, had been wonderful. I knew I should apply for my test, but I was pathetically stupid. I already had a full bloody licence so they could stick it! As I've already said, talk about cutting off your nose to spite your face.

Most of the JW outings were a similar kind of affair. Best of all, however, were the cinema trips and parties. In the dark of the cinema, nobody could see us holding hands, while at the parties we were allowed to dance together. It seems absurd now, but how was it that most of the congregation – particularly the Elders – didn't suspect we were an item?

It was about this time that Mark became my best friend amongst the Witnesses (the boat mob were a different matter) and he'd already been close friends with Jo. Not only were we now good buddies, he'd also passed his test on his CD175. It had been his second attempt. On the first try, when the examiner had told him he'd failed he'd taken in his stride... NOT.

"Bollocks, I can't have!" he'd cried furiously. And he always insisted that this first performance had been perfect, while his second had been terrible. Yet that time he'd passed. Go figure.

But from then on, if the three of us went anywhere together or as part of a crowd, Jo would go with him with me following behind staring at *Jo's* behind, if you know what I mean. Lovely.

# 4: BROKEN BONES

I've spoken previously about how my relationship with the Boat Mob was getting closer. Indeed, there were outings with them which were far more exciting than those with my religious friends. We would go for rides just for the sake of going for a ride. We would sit in the Boat chatting and drinking with our bikes lined up outside in the car park. And we would also go and sit in the Little Chef on the A2.

A race past the Chef took place most weeks because it was vital to know whose bike was the fastest. As wicked as mine was, I never seemed to win any races. It was always close, but I never seemed to be able to edge in front of the other RDs. Unfortunately, my time with the lads from the Boat was still limited by JW meetings and of course, seeing Jo.

There was one Friday night when just Smiffy and I went to the Central Hotel's disco together. We had a pretty good time too. We both managed to get a couple of dances in with some pretty girls (which pricked my conscience a bit) and Smiffy even managed to play tonsil tennis with one of them.

Now I was fairly careful about drinking and driving, but just one pint spread over a whole evening seemed a bit measly. But then while I was at the bar to get my one and only pint of lager, the bloke beside me ordered a barley wine. I'd never heard of the drink before, so I watched curiously as it arrived. The bloke was presented with a small bottle and a glass. I watched as he poured it and wow, it looked just like beer. Brilliant!

"Barley wine, please," I said trying to sound like it was my usual tipple.

The barman gave me the usual odd look because it was pretty obvious I was underage. Even so, my drink was soon placed in front of me. I was a bit taken back that this tiny drink cost as much as a pint, but I handed the money over (about 35p) then poured the amber liquid into the glass. Cautiously, I raised it to my lips and tasted it. It really did taste like beer, but with a bit more bite. And being such a small amount, I could drink a few of them and stay sober. The flaw in my cunning plan only became obvious when the disco was over and Smiffy and I stepped out into the cold night air. If his famously quick reflexes hadn't caught me, I'd have wound up flat on my face.

"You alright?" he asked.

"Yeah fine," I slurred in reply.

He took me at my word, and we climbed aboard our bikes. Our RDs burst into life and simultaneously we snicked them into gear. His blue RD250C took off with me following close behind. Now Smiffy was one of the quickest riders I've ever known, and it soon became apparent that this was going to be a race. I tucked in behind him as we screamed through the narrow streets of the big estate. I was rather surprised that I was staying with him. We flew along, braking hard as we swung through the corners, our footpegs folding as they scraped the tarmac in a shower of sparks. Then it all went wrong.

To my alcohol clouded eyes, it looked as though the road went straight ahead, but what I thought was a road was actually someone's drive. In reality, the road turned sharply to the right. Smiffy's sudden brake light took me completely by surprise. I hauled on my brakes, but it was too late. My front wheel locked up and down the bike went. It bounced off Smiffy's bike and then crashed into the kerb. In the quiet, late-night streets the crash made one hell of a racket. Several front doors opened, and a couple of people came running over.

"It's all right," one lady said. "I've called an ambulance."

"We don't need an ambulance!" Smiffy cried urgently. He knew that with an ambulance would come the police, accompanied of course by the dreaded breathalyser.

"I do need one," I said from underneath the bike and holding up my right hand. "I've broken my pinkie!" Sure enough, my little finger was bent at a most excruciating angle. Luckily, barley wine proved to be a most effective pain killer.

"You don't need an ambulance for a f***ing broken finger!"

"I do," I replied gazing blearily at the offending digit. "It's broken really bad."

"Oh for crying out loud!" Smiffy cried in exasperation as he picked my bike up, freeing my legs. "You don't need a f***ing ambulance!"

But I was determined. An ambulance was exactly what I *did* need, or so I thought. "I do," I slurred emphatically.

By the time he'd parked my bike on one kindly person's drive, we could hear a distant siren (yes they really did come that quickly back then). Smiffy gave me a sympathetic look then got back on his bike ready to shoot off if the old bill turned up. I believe he was a bit over the limit himself.

I can't understand how unbelievably lucky I was; It was just the ambulance. No police arrived at all. An ambulance man carefully (and painfully) removed my glove and nodded sagely. "Yup, that's broken alright." Talk about stating the bleedin' obvious. "Hop in the back and we'll run you to the hospital."

I could see Smiffy shaking his head in disbelief, but he didn't desert me.

"I'll meet you at the A&E," he called, his voice muffled from beneath his lid.

"Yeah, see you there."

"Ten minutes later I walked into the amazingly empty waiting room (oh how different things are now) to find Smiffy already there waiting for me.

It only took about ten minutes for me to be seen but it seemed much longer with Smiffy's non-stop scolding and piss-taking. After my hand was x-rayed, I went back to the waiting room for more piss-taking. Eventually an Asian doctor came out with the x-ray in his hand. He held it up and scrutinised it carefully. So did I. I could easily see where the bone was snapped because there was a nice gap where the finger pointed off to the side at an odd angle.

"Ah yes," the doctor said rather contemptuously. "You are having a very slight fracture here. I'll get a nurse to bind it for you."

*A slight fracture!* I thought incredulously. *It's effing snapped in half!*

I was quickly taken to a booth where a not-so-nice nurse gave my poor little pinkie a bit of a tug then proceeded to wrap a couple of miles of sticking plaster around it. I was extremely heroic and didn't cry out, but that was probably more to do with the barley wine than my bravery. Once it was done, I wandered back out to the waiting room, and after I procured a sick note, Smiffy gave me a lift home.

As you know, I worked in the clothes shop, Burtons, and having Saturday's off was not allowed. But I was signed off for a week so that was that. Even so, my dad gave me hell. As far as he was concerned, a broken finger was *not* a good enough excuse to take a week off work, and I was therefore skiving.

A few years later he apologised profusely when he broke his thumb. Yes, he too took a sickie, and for a good fortnight at that!

It was Ivor and Smiffy who picked my bike up and brought it home. When it came back, I stood there looking at it forlornly. But as it turned out, it wasn't too badly damaged. The offside rear indicator was hanging down, suspended by its wires, and the handlebars seemed to be bent. But it was just twisted forks which were easily sorted by holding the front wheel between my knees and giving the bars a good tug. I 'fixed' the indicator by wrapping it up in insulating tape; a sad parody of my broken finger's wrapping.

The thick plaster did cause one particular problem. I was to keep it on for about six weeks, but there was no way I could get my glove on. How was I going to get to work when my sicknote ran out? The answer was brutally simple: I just cut the pinkie finger off my glove. Problem solved.

You know that finger never did set straight. Even forty odd years later it points out at a slight angle, and when it gets really cold, it bloody hurts.

There was one good lesson learned from this tragic incident. I didn't drink and drive again – well not to excess, anyway. For many decades now, I've been *extremely* careful drink-wise. And I take a dim view of those who do get pissed and get behind the wheel – or handlebars. If you do, it'll probably be more than just a broken pinkie; it could be someone's life.

# 5: PUBS AND PUNCTURES

When I was at school I had two very good friends, Allan and Tommy. Both were very intelligent and in the top classes, excelling in all of them and especially in maths. Although I trounced them in English, I always did struggle with the numbers game. At least I felt I did, for although I was only one tier down from them in the subject, it had never come easy to me. That had all changed in our final year when another good friend, Philmore, gave me a few useful tips. Suddenly, everything clicked. Philmore and I were both moved up from the CSE class to the hallowed heights of the GCE O level one. Allan and Tommy welcomed me with open arms, I on the other hand found myself struggling again. So I asked to be dropped back down to the CSE group. Let's face it, better to be a big fish in a little pond, than the other way round. To my mind it worked out okay in the end; I gained an easy grade one CSE, which was considered equivalent to a grade C GCE. Grade C was considered pretty good in the difficult O level exams. A bit different from today when anything less than a grade A star plus plus plus with bells on is considered a derisory failure!

Now although Tommy and Allan were both swots, they were very sporting. Whether it be football, cricket, or tennis, they were brilliant. Although not as good as them, I wasn't too bad either. So we spent many an hour playing tennis together or kicking a ball around. By the time we were seventeen, I discovered another thing they were good at: pubbing. Suddenly I had another circle of friends straining at the strict bonds of life as a Jehovah's Witness. We went many places. The Admiral Beaty, The Central Hotel's Friday night disco, and best of all, since Tommy worked for the council, the NALGO club.

The only problem with all this was that neither one of my old school friends possessed a bike, and nor did they want too. Shame on them! So I used to ride my RD down to Tommy's house and sling it in his back garden. Then, with Tommy, Allan, and another friend, Mick, we would walk to wherever we were going to that night. Sounds boring but we always had a good laugh as we strolled to our designated watering hole.

Since I had to ride the mile or two from Tommy's to my place, I was always careful about how much I drank. Didn't want another broken pinkie, doncha know. To be honest, I really didn't hold my drink too well. In fact, one sniff of a wine gum and I was under the table. No wonder the barley wine had affected me so badly. So a couple of pints was the absolute most I'd allow myself, figuring the walk back to Tommy's would help to clear my head.

But no matter how much I enjoyed these nights out, the best part of the evening was getting on the bike for the ride home. Sometimes I took the long way round because...well, who could resist. The sound of that wonderful two stroke twin engine and the sudden surge as it hit the power band was more intoxicating than the beer.

One night, however, my lovely ride home was spoilt by one minor flaw: a sodding puncture. No, not as I was swinging through the corners or howling inconsiderately through the streets of our estate. I was thankfully spared that awful fate. No, we got back to Tommy's house and there it was. The rear tyre was as flat as a sheet of tissue paper (a pancake is far too inflated for this analogy). It was way too dark to sod around with it that night, so there was nothing for it but a long walk home. Good job it was a Saturday night. It gave me all Sunday to fix it. *And* I was grateful to have an excuse to avoid the increasingly tedious JW meeting.

If you've read *Sixteener Special* you'll recall my other puncture experiences. So this time, I was prepared. I'd heard about this wonderful item called Finilec, a version of today's Tyre Weld. You know the stuff, an aerosol can of foamy goo that pumps up the tyre and seals the puncture at the same time. I'd bought some a while ago just in case. So early the next morning I arrived back at Tommy's with this miracle cure in my hand.

I swear I followed the instructions; I know I did. I found the offending nail, pulled it out, had the hole facing the ground, carefully attached the little hose, and then pushed the button. The foam went in and... nothing! I could have screamed with frustration. In the end I had to revert to the old-fashioned puncture repair kit. I was pretty good at getting the patches to stick, but after pinching the tube three or four times getting the tyre on, there was only one patch left. I stuck it on but then just stood pathetically looking at the wheel. I just couldn't bring myself to continue. What if I pinched the tube again? The only viable option then would be a new tube, which meant being late – very late – for work the next day. I flinched at the thought of my dad's reaction to that idea, but what else could I do?

My salvation came from a most surprising and rather embarrassing source. Tommy's younger brother pushed me aside and before I could ask for the ground to swallow me up, it was done. Happy days. But then came an even bigger problem. Should I go over to Jo's that afternoon or go and see the boy's up the Boat? In the end I decided that my poor bruised ego needed pampering, so I plumped for the former.

You'd think that all things considered, I'd take it easy as I swung through the lanes to her house. Nope, with total disregard for the umpteen patches on the inner tube, I hammered my wicked 250 all the way. Twice I sent up a shower of sparks as my foot pegs touched down. I say the bike was wicked for a good reason. It was! It seemed to have a will of its own, possessing me, and twisting my wrist, whacking the throttle against the stop. Spooky...

# 6: FRUSTRATION AND ODD DECISIONS

I mentioned back in chapter two about my RD's propensity to drop onto one cylinder in the rain. Despite copious amounts of WD40, the problem was occurring more and more often. Then, one fine and sunny Saturday morning in early October, the damned thing did it again. I was dumbfounded. It had been dry the day before and nobody had so much as spat on the ground near it since. Nevertheless, I gave it the usual quirt of WD40 and... Nothing. My beloved and wicked 250 twin was now an oversized, not so wicked, 125 single!

I was still fiddling around with it when my dad and stepmother, Gwen, walked out to the garage.

"What's the matter with it?" my dad asked.

"It's only firing on one pot," I replied frustratedly – which of course meant nothing to my mechanically uneducated dad.

"Well you can't sit here messing around with it. You need to get going or you'll be late for work."

"But..."

"You can't be late," he replied in that quiet, steely, *you're a bloody idiot Steve* voice he always used when I pissed him off. "It's Saturday."

"But it's not working properly!" I protested.

"Can you ride it like that?"

"Yeah, sort of. But it'll go like a slug and it won't tick over."

"Does it matter how fast it goes?" Gwen put in. "As long as it gets you there, there's no problem."

"But the tick over."

"I'm sure you'll find a way to work around it," dad said firmly.

I muttered something unprintable under my breath. I doubted he even knew what a tick over was. But still, I shoved my lid on in a suitably huffy manner and jumped on the ailing bike. "I just hope it bloody gets me there," I said angrily as I stamped it into gear. I then gave it a good bit of throttle and pulled away.

The ride to Chatham wasn't too bad I suppose. Even with only half the engine working it was faster than my old fizzy, but boy it was tedious and frustrating.

Then, after three or four miles, pot number two decided to join the party. I breathed a sigh of relief and slipped through the light, Saturday morning traffic. I tried to forget all about it, but it was at the back of my mind all morning. I couldn't for the life of me work out what was causing the problem. There was nothing for it but to change the plugs and caps. So at lunchtime I walked up to Grays, the big bike shop up the road. I was so concerned about the problem that I didn't even nip into the showroom to drool over the bikes.

I had just enough time left on my lunch hour to swap everything over before getting back on the shop floor. It was a busy afternoon so serving all the many customers took my mind off things a bit. But come six o'clock when the doors closed, I hurried out to my poorly, gleaming bronze beauty and anxiously prodded the kickstart. Whing, whing, it went first try. I let out a deep breath of profound relief. I knew I'd fixed it. The new plugs and caps had solved the problem.

And I was right – for about three days that is. Then once again, I was left with a 125 single on the way to work. This time the second pot didn't kick in until I was almost at the shop. Again, the bloody thing ran perfectly all the way home.

The problem happened a couple of more times and nobody I asked could come up with a solution, although someone up the boat (I forget who) suggested I try new coils. So on my next day off I went to the little bike shop in Gravesend where my dad had bought the Fizz for me.

"How much!?" I cried in horror when I was told the price.

"That's each," the shop owner said flatly. "And I'll have to order them in since we don't carry them in stock."

"I'll have to think about it," I said in a daze. I walked numbly out to the bike and just stood there looking at it for what seemed like an age. Then I remembered what Martin had said when I'd informed him of my problem.

"It's a two stroke," he'd said smugly. "Should have got a four stroke."

That really pissed me off since he'd been the one who'd found the bike in the paper and had been the one who'd persuaded my old man that it was a good buy. Even so a plan started to form in my head. Would he let me PX it against a Honda? I remembered that as far as brand new was concerned I was limited to an RD200 and not the RD250. So if I could only have had a 200, what if I could have a CB200 Honda. In a 200 shootout test I'd seen in one of my bike magazines, they'd tested the RD200, the CB200, and the Suzuki GT185 against each other. And all round, they'd rated the Honda top of the bunch. And despite the RD's scorching performance blowing the other two into the weeds, it had come last!

To further my idea, the next Monday I rode up to the Chatham bike shop in my lunch hour. I walked into the showroom and had a good look over the green and black CB200 on display. I sat on it, stroked it, and sniffed it. Could I really drop down from an RD250 to one of these? I took a deep breath and decided that I could. I was so frustrated with the RD that the Honda's bullet proof reliability was more than a little enticing.

"Are you okay there?" the salesman asked a bit dismissively. He'd often seen me looking around and he clearly wasn't too impressed with the way I was all over the bike.

"Yeah," I replied sounding keen. "I was thinking of buying it."

Instantly, the salesman's attitude changed. "I see," he said, mentally rubbing his hands together. "So can I be of assistance any assistance?"

"Um, yes please. I'd like to know how much you'll give me in part exchange for my bike."

"Right," he said warily. "And what bike do you have?"

"An RD250B," I replied.

"And you want to swap it for a CB200? That's rather unusual."

I suddenly realised just how unusual a swap it was. He was clearly a little suspicious. "Oh it's just too much for me," I lied. "I want something a bit easier to handle."

"Ah," he said knowingly. "I know what you mean. Is your bike outside?"

"Yeah, it is."

So we both went out to the bike and he gave it a thorough going over. I winced when he noticed the taped on rear indicator.

"What happened here," he asked suspiciously.

"Oh, I was rolling it off the centre stand and it just got away from me," I lied, the excuse flashing into my brain.

"A bit heavy, eh?" he said nodding sagely as he looked my thin gangly frame up and down.

"Yeah, just a bit. That's why I want the 200. It's a bit lighter. And it doesn't have a fierce power band."

"Hmm..." he murmured standing up straight and giving me an apologetic look. "I'm afraid I can only offer you three hundred."

I tried my best to look disappointed but inside my heart was turning somersaults of joy. I'd only paid £275 for it three months ago.

"I see," I said carefully. I blew out my cheeks thoughtfully. "Well I suppose that will have to do."

"And how were you thinking of paying the difference? Will you be needing finance?"

"Oh no, it'll be cash. I just need to get my parents to agree to it all – which shouldn't be a problem," I added quickly seeing the disappointed look on his face. "I'll be in tomorrow or the next day to sort it all out."

And that was it. He wrote all the details out for me to show my dad and gave me a brochure. Now I just needed to persuade him what a good idea it was.

"So what's the matter with your own bike?" dad asked with a deep frown. I'd broached the subject after work as carefully as I could, but I could see he wasn't at all happy.

"You've seen the way it keeps messing around," I said. "It's just not reliable enough."

"It still manages to get you to work every day."

"Yeah, but for how long? And anyway, it's much faster than I need, and I want something that does more to the gallon."

"And this Honda 200 does more does it?"

"Oh loads more," I gushed. "About twice as much."

"What about selling yours. You did nothing to sell your moped and I'm not having two big bikes hanging around taking up space."

"No problem, they said I could part exchange it."

"And how much money will I lose doing that?"

I grinned, "Nothing. In fact they offered twenty-five quid more than we paid for it. Here look, he wrote it all out for me."

"Hmm..." he said taking the piece of paper and stroking his chin. "I'll have a chat with Gwen and we'll think about it."

And think they did. But only for that evening. He collared me next morning and smiled. "We think it's nice to see you being sensible for a change," he said putting a cheque in my hand. "When will you be able to pick it up?"

"I don't know. I'll go in lunch time and sort it all out. It shouldn't be too long though. They've got one in stock."

So true to my word, I went in that afternoon and gave them the cheque. "When can I pick it up," I asked.

"When do want it?"

"Well, tomorrow's my day off so I don't suppose I could get it then, could I?"

The salesman scratched his head. "That doesn't give us much... Hold on, I'll see if the workshop can fit in the PDI this afternoon." He picked up the phone and rang through to the workshop. After a bit of to-and-fro, he smiled and thanked the person on the other end.

"Yes," he said after hanging up. "Tomorrow will be fine."

"What time," I asked eagerly.

"Well, we have to register it and tax it at the post office first, so about eleven to eleven-thirty should be okay."

"Brilliant!" I said happily. "Thank you so much."

"No problem," he said reaching across the desk and shaking my hand. "We'll see you then."

That evening, my dad took the news pretty well. "That's quick," he said as I informed him that I'd be picking up the bike tomorrow morning.

I excitedly explained how they'd had one in stock and had managed to do the pre-delivery inspection that afternoon. "It's green and black. It looks really nice."

"Yes," he sighed. "You showed me the brochure yesterday."

I decided not to go out on the RD that evening – just in case. I didn't want an accident to spoil the brilliant trade in price they'd given me. Next morning I was up bright and early, considering it was my day off. In fact, I set off for the bike shop not long after nine o'clock. Since I wasn't due at the bike shop until eleven, I was going to be ridiculously early. In fact, I arrived at about half past nine.

I wandered into the showroom and the salesman gave me a big smile. "You're keen," he said strolling over to me.

"I know. I thought I'd get here early just in case it was ready."

"Oh the bike's ready," he said brightly. We're just waiting for someone to go to the post office and register it etcetera."

"Oh, right."

"Don't worry," he said reassuringly. "Tom's just tying up a loose end in the workshop. He'll be here soon."

I nodded. "That's all right, I'll just look around. I love seeing all the bikes."

"I know you do," he said with a grin. "I've seen you in here often enough."

As I looked at all the bikes, I wandered over to where the CB200 had been the day before. My green one was gone and had been replaced by a red one. Hmmm. I really did prefer the green. Good job....

At that moment my eye was drawn to a flash of colour a few feet away. It was a bright orange RD200DX. As if in a trance I walked slowly over to it. It seemed to be calling out to me as if I were a sailor and it was a siren. I gulped as I looked at its sleek, coffin tank adorned with those wonderful black and white speed blocks. Then there was that cheeky little orange tail attached to the back of the seat. I looked back at the Honda. Somehow the clocks on it seemed cheap in comparison to the Yam's. And the switchgear. The Yamaha's were slick and modern looking – it even had self-cancelling indicators for crying out loud. In comparison, the Honda's switchgear looked like they were made of 19th century Bakelite!

I suddenly made a momentous decision. I walked back over to the salesman. "I've changed my mind," I said firmly. "I want the RD200."

"What? No, that's not possible; everything's already been sorted."

"But I don't want the poxy Honda, I want the RD200."

"But..."

"Please," I said beseechingly, giving him my best doe-eyed pleading look. "Surely there's a way? They're the same price after all."

He stared at me thoughtfully. "Are you sure?" he asked earnestly.

"Positive!"

"You won't change your mind again?"

"Nope."

"Hmm... Well just hang on a minute and I'll see what I can do. I'm not promising anything, mind."

I nodded hopefully, crossing my fingers as he picked up the phone. I listened to the one-sided conversation with bated breath. "Hi Tom. Listen, you know that RD200 that's due for collection tomorrow? Have you done the PDI on it yet? So it's all ready to go? Okay. Why? Well the gentleman's here to pick up the CB200 you prepped yesterday, but he's changed his mind and wants the RD instead. Yeah, I know.... I know but he's pretty insistent. Well he's not due in until late afternoon tomorrow, so I'd be really grateful if you can prep another RD for him before he gets here. Really? You're a star Tom."

He hung up and beamed at me. "You're a lucky lad. We've got an RD200 all ready to go. Now you're sure you're not going to change your mind again, are you? You're absolutely certain that this is what you want?"

"Positive."

"Okay then. Tom's sending Jack straight over, so he'll be here in a minute. He'll take the details up to the post office and when he gets back, you'll be all ready to go."

As it turned out, I was all ready to go just thirty minutes later. I bid my wicked RD250 goodbye and set off on the little 200. And I was smitten from the start. And I mean start. The little Yam actually had an electric start – or 'pansy-kicker'.

The soft, smooth cackle of the exhaust note promised good things to come, but I didn't dare let it rev too high. I was going to run it in more carefully than any bike had been run in before. So I settled at around forty mph all the way along the Rochester Road. And I didn't take it a whisker over 4,500 revs when accelerating through the gears. Very slow, but even so, the motor didn't feel laboured. Just sweet and crisp. I decided that I'd only do fifty miles at this speed, then do about a hundred miles at five thousand, four hundred miles at five and a half, then increase the revs by five hundred every fifty miles. Of course, once it had done about four hundred miles, I'd give it a quick blast of throttle, just to prevent the bores from glazing.

I couldn't wait to tell my dad about the stroke of luck I'd had swapping my order.

"You bloody lied to me!" he shouted angrily.

I was aghast. How could he accuse me of such a huge lie? Yes, I'd told him the occasional fib, but to make up a story like this? How could he think such a thing?

"No I didn't," I cried. "They just happened to have a Yamaha ready to go but not registered yet, and..."

"You really expect me to believe that nonsense? That's not how it works!"

"But, honestly, that's exactly what happened."

"Huh!" he scoffed bitterly. "You bloody tricked me. You were getting the Yamaha all along."

By now I was almost in tears. "Honestly, I didn't trick you. It's just when I saw the two bikes side by side this morning, the RD200 was just so much better. And they were really good there. They went right out of their way to..."

"Rubbish. Just get out of my sight. You've really disappointed me."

I didn't know whether to be upset or angry. So without any dinner, I left the house, and after a quick and disappointing stop at Martin's house – he thought I was a bloody idiot – I rode over to Jo's. At least there I would get some joy.

"It's all right, I suppose," she said looking the bike over. "I prefer your two-fifty though."

Sometimes in this life, what seems like a lucky break can cause all manner of disappointment. I just hoped the little orange firecracker would be worth it.

# 7: SLOW AND STEADY

Running in has always been a source of frustration for bikers. Many follow the routine set out in the manual, while others haven't quite got the patience to rigidly keep to the manufacturer's recommended schedule. So, after starting out with good intentions, they soon find themselves opening their bikes up before the motor's fully bedded in. I've known a couple, however, who just couldn't give a stuff. From the moment they first turn the key, they're off like a guided missile, redlining their poor little beast mercilessly. As I've said, I had decided to be extra careful with my new, orange RD200. I was going to be even more meticulous than I had been with my FS1E. I was going to ensure that it was the best run-in bike on the planet!

As I described in the previous chapter, my ride home from the bike shop had been incredibly cautious. Not exceeding 4,500 revs through the gears and sitting at forty mph in top which equated to around the 4,000 rpm mark. I did a quick calculation in my head. If 4,000 rpm equated to forty, then 9,000 rpm would be around ninety. Excellent. Okay, I surmised, if you give a little leeway for speedo inaccuracy, then the eighty-seven recorded in all the bike mags sounded just right. I grinned to myself, delighted at the patience I was about to display.

As I said earlier, after the row with old man, I'd gone round to Martin's to show off my new beast. His disdain had been palpable. I felt as though he'd just punched me in the stomach. Which was why, with my ego in tatters, I'd made my way over to my beloved girlfriend. I took the longer, winding way which had always made my Fizzy feel fast, and to my delight, it had a similar effect on the 200. Except it was much better since the 200's headlight actually managed to light up the road, and the bike handled a bit better too. It augured well for the things to come.

The disappointing reaction to my new steed had one very strange effect. For some reason it made me far more likely to attend the JW meetings at the Kingdom Hall, as well as the Tuesday evening book study. So had the little bike stirred up a religious fervour in my soul? Like hell it had; I just couldn't face all the taunts from my friends at the Boat. If Martin *and* Mark had displayed such contempt, what on Earth would the reaction be with those up the Boat?

So I left off my association with the Boat Mob, and rode mainly with Mark, and sometimes Martin. But since Tommy and Allan didn't know a Z1 from a Puch Maxi, I still managed the occasional jaunt to the pub with them, safe in the knowledge that they wouldn't take the piss.

Despite my patience, the running in procedure seemed to take forever. I followed my schedule to the letter, slowly letting the available revs increase until I could let myself ride it flat out. But despite the increase in revs as the miles rolled by, I still never gave it full throttle, and I never went above sixty in top gear, until...

I was on my way to work when the trip meter clicked over to show the magic thousand miles. Unfortunately, I was wending my way through the Saturday morning traffic at the time, so I couldn't open it up. But if I went home via the A2, I could give it full chat past the Little Chef. Would it hit eighty-seven or would it reach ninety? Or would the discrepancy I'd notice between the rev counter and the speedo blow the whole thing out the water? You see I knew the physics and the maths of gear ratios. I'd devoured such things in all the bike magazines I'd read (pretty much every publication on the market).

Today was going to be the day to find out if I was right in my calculations. You see, with each rise in revs I'd allowed myself in top gear, the rpm to mph correlation had drifted further and further out. Sixty should have arrived six thousand revs, but the rev counter actually read 6,300. Hmmm. That would make it around eighty-five at the redline. But the proof of the pudding would be in the eating.

At last the six o'clock closing time came round, and as usual, I was away in an instant. I was almost trembling with anticipation as I finally hit the imitation motorway which was the A2. I climbed the initial hill at a steady seventy, amazed at how easily the little 200 had reached and maintained the speed limit. Then I crested the rise and it was downhill on the run past the Chef.

I didn't lay flat on the tank. Unlike my Boat Mob brethren, I still felt too self-conscious to perform such antics – which is probably why I could never win on the two-fifty. As soon as I'd crested the hill, I nailed the throttle wide open. Okay, I might not have done the flat on the tank routine, but I did allow myself to crouch down a bit.

As soon as I slammed the throttle open, the bike seemed to shoot forward amazingly quickly. The speedo rose in a very satisfying manner until it peaked at...

*Eighty-one?* I cried in dismay. *Eighty flaming one!* Surely it was a mistake. But no, I was definitely sitting at the 9,000 rpm redline at a sodding pathetic eighty-one miles per sodding hour! The poxy CB200 I'd spurned would have gone faster than this. It seemed my careful and extended running procedure was all in vain. My terrible disappointment was unbounded. I decided there and then that it would be a long time before I let anyone know how slow the bike was. The bike, on the other hand, had other ideas. It would be remarkably soon when the little firecracker declared just how damned *quick* it was!

# 8: CHRISTMAS, SNOW, AND ICE

It was by now well into December, and Christmas was fast approaching. Not that that meant anything to the Jehovah's Witnesses; to them Christmas is considered a pagan celebration and one to be avoided at all costs.

Except...

Yeah, you've guessed it. Despite being a JW, I found the celebrations a little too hard to avoid. My dad and Gwen as well as my older sister, Angela, were certainly *not* Witnesses. Anything but. My dad was a devout and often outspoken atheist, and although Gwen tended to keep her thoughts to herself, Ange would take the piss relentlessly. So Christmas was quite a big thing in our house. Okay, I declined the opportunity to receive presents, but I did struggle not to get involved in the spirit of the thing – especially when going down the pub with Tommy and Allan.

Christmas Eve that year was on a Friday – and yes, I'd had to go to work! But Friday was my usual night out with Tom and Allan so off to the jolly old pub we went. And what a time we had. As the evening went on and the booze flowed copiously, so did the merry mood of everyone there. Yes, I was still careful with my drink, but the atmosphere was intoxicating, nonetheless. There was singing and laughter, and best of all, that most evil of Christmas things to be avoided, mistletoe, was liberally hung all around the place. And many a tipsy girl made herself available by standing strategically under it. I'm sorry to say that, despite the strictures placed upon me by JW rules, I couldn't resist the occasional snog – sorry Jo.

It was this Christmas which caused me to really contemplate my religious values. I was getting totally fed up with all the rules and regulations that made my life so boring. I liked most of the people at the Kingdom Hall, and I still kind of believed most of it, but the already wide cracks in my faith took a heavy blow that Yuletide. And I knew Jo wasn't as devout as she appeared – she liked nooky too much for a start! So the spirit of Christmas was doing its very best to open those cracks even wider. But I still kept going to the meetings. I guess I was what today's ex-Witnesses call PIMO. Physically In, Mentally Out.

\* \* \*

As winter grew dark and cold, January gave us a bit of snow. Not a lot in the corner of the UK where I lived, but it was pretty widespread elsewhere. And even though we just got a short and rather light downfall, it did cause a few problems on the roads. But I was a good rider and the little RD200 was a gem on the slippery stuff. The engine was remarkably flexible, and its light weight and good steering made it easy to control on the icy roads. Even so there were a couple of awkward moments.

The first occurred when the snow had cleared and the roads well salted – although not so much on my estate. I breathed a sigh of relief that morning when I reached the Rochester Road to find it as clear as could be. Wet, but not a sign of snow or slush. So I gave the bike a bit of throttle and settled down to usual sixty to sixty-five mph. Then as I rounded the first bend, I saw it. A big lump of rough, compacted snow. It wasn't a problem for cars of course since it was slap bang in the middle of the road. I, unfortunately, had no chance of avoiding it. Before I could say, *shit!* I was on it.

I swear it was the bike. I just know it spoke to me – well kind of anyway.

"Relax," the voice that wasn't a voice said. "I've got this."

So I relaxed and just let the bike do its thing. The snow wasn't just compacted and extremely slippery, it wasn't in the least bit flat. It was cursed with all kinds of lumps and ruts. I was sure I was in for a sixty mph coming together with the road. But the RD was having none of it. I kept the throttle as neutral as possible – neither decelerating nor accelerating – and just let it all happen.

The bike slipped and wriggled and shimmied, and then it was over. The bike had taken it in its stride as if it hadn't been at all dangerous, just a great bit of fun. My brown underpants, on the other hand, disagreed!

The next incident wasn't caused by snow but by an excruciatingly cold morning which was even more difficult to manage. It was, however, a great deal less dangerous. I awoke to the roads being covered in Ice. Smooth, slippery, and all over the tarmac. The streets were nothing less than a skating rink. Seriously, it was frozen everywhere from kerb to kerb. Getting the bike out of the garage was difficult enough. At any moment I was likely to do a fine impression of a ballerina – or the male equivalent, whatever that is.

Gingerly I pulled away – in second gear as I'd read in one magazine which has slipped my mind. I crept along at a very timid five mph knowing that just a touch of the brakes would send me and the bike sliding gracefully up the road. I reached the junction with Thong Lane where we used to race our mopeds and delicately turned into it.

I hadn't gone more than a couple of hundred yards when a prat in a BMW came up behind me. The stupid, middle class, German auto loving wanker then proceeded to honk his horn and flash his lights continuously. He was clearly in a hurry and took great offence at my careful five mph progress. He actually wanted me to pull over and let him pass.

"In your dreams, arsehole," I muttered angrily.

After a short while the plonker could take it no more. With a loud and pronged blast of his horn, he shot past giving his flash motor the beans.

It was inevitable. He was barely past when he lost it. I laughed out loud as his precious bee-em spun a beautifully elegant three-hundred-and-sixty-degree spin. Lucky for him, he came to rest facing the right way. I shut my throttle, hoping he would get going before I needed to touch my back brake. Fortunately, he did and proceeded to crawl down the road at a heady *five* miles per hour – just like sensible old me.

I couldn't resist flashing my headlight a couple of times, accompanied by a few toots of my horn, naturally.

That was pretty much it that winter as far as scares went. It was however bitterly cold, and I still only wore my suit trousers. Every day, by the time I got to work my legs were red raw with the cold. But I still refused to buy any waterproofs or leathers. Yeah, hard as nails me – as if. Just stupid more like. But not altogether stupid because I hadn't bought the Honda. More and more I was coming to respect the remarkable abilities of this plucky little orange fireball.

# 9: HEARTBREAK AND A FALL FROM GRACE

February came and went with the same old routine. It was kind of a schizophrenic life, I suppose. On the one hand I had the appearance of a devout Jehovah's Witness, while on the other, I was spending Friday nights at the pub or in the disco with Tommy, Allan, and, Mick. Occasionally though, Jo and I would go somewhere interesting with Mark, my best JW friend. He was very much a good friend by now and was a lot less rigid than Martin. And boy could he make that anachronistic old CD175 fly. At one point he'd been out with Martin and had clocked a ton on his speedo down the steep hill on the A2 known as the Swanscombe Cutting – and that was no bullshit! The fact that his speedo was wildly optimistic, however, made the true speed about eighty-five according to Martin's clock; but that's still trucking on for that type of bike. Faster than my bike's poxy eighty-one, I thought sourly. At times like that I really did regret not getting the Honda 200.

I was still avoiding the Boat Mob as best I could, but since I rode past the boat two, or even three or four times a day, I knew I'd been spotted several times. So I knew the news of my demotion from a 250 to a 200 would have spread. And because I was avoiding their company, I was missing out on the races past the Chef and other balls-out thrashes we (now they) tended to engage in. Consequently, I was pretty much unaware of how my little RD's performance was improving. I did, however, take the long way home from work one day, just to give it a blast past the Chef. I was gob-smacked when the rev counter needle pulled into the red giving me a top speed of a solid eighty-four. Much better than its original eighty-one.

March went very much the same as February except for one thing: Jo appeared to become more and more distant. She was now working in a lighting showroom in Gravesend which perhaps had something to do with it. But I was damned if I knew how it did. Then in April we went to an Assembly – which was a special meeting where lots of JW congregations gather to 'associate' and get 'encouragement' from the JW Governing Body.

As usual, I met up with Jo and sat down beside her. To my horror she was as cold as ice. And her friend

Elaine seemed to be encouraging it. I found out the cause a week or so later.

"Sorry Steve," she said when I met her in her lunch break. "I think we need to take a break."

"What?" I said dumbfounded. "Why do we need to do that? What's wrong?"

At first she wouldn't say, but my increasingly desperate pleas eventually ground out the truth. She'd been seeing one of the blokes at her shop (well the other Gravesend branch to be more accurate) for a few weeks, and as she didn't want to two time me any longer, she was giving me the old heave-ho.

I was completely devastated. I just couldn't understand it. How could she do such a thing? We'd kind of had an unspoken agreement that we'd spend the rest of our lives together. And now this. I went home in a numb daze, but after sitting staring blankly at my bedroom wall, the reality hit me that I would never see the only girl I'd ever loved again. Like a big girl, I broke down and wept bitter tears for several hours. Then a steely resolve filled my heart. Sod tonight's meeting at the Kingdom Hall! I did the only sensible thing I could do. I searched the phone book and found the number of my old friend, Tracy. If you've read *Sixteener Special*, you'll recall that she was the one who'd burnt her leg on my Fizzy's exhaust.

"Hi Tracy, it's Steve," I said as brightly as I could manage.

To my amazement, she immediately recognised my voice. "Hello," she said warily. "This is a surprise."

"I suppose it is," I said with a chuckle. "Erm... I was wondering... erm..."

"What?"

"Will you go out with me?" I eventually blurted out.

"I thought you were going out with, oh, what's her name, Jo?"

"Oh, that's well over," I said casually.

"Really? Well of course I'll go out with you. You didn't really need to ask – you should have known that."

I breathed a sigh of relief.

"Tell you what, Steve, come round my house now. You can stay for dinner and then maybe go for a walk."

And that's exactly what I did. I'd never been in her house before and it was quite an experience. They actually had *two* televisions in the lounge – one on top of the other. Turned out her dad liked to watch BBC1 and ITV at the same time! Weird, eh?

I really liked Tracy, and despite her incredibly foul-mouthed language, we got on so well it was spooky. And yet, there didn't seem to be any romantic spark. No matter how she tried to go further than a good snog, I just couldn't bring myself to engage in it all.

My heart was still bleeding from the knife Jo had mercilessly rammed into it. Eventually I broke Tracy's heart by dumping her for her friend, Mandy.

Now Mandy was a little prettier than Tracy (who was rather stunning in her own right) but what really drew me to her was she had a figure that was very much like Jo's. Like me, she too had just been dumped after a long-term relationship, so we understood each other pretty well. And neither of us felt any pressure to engage in nooky. So we didn't.

One interesting thing to mention. When the guys up the Boat eventually heard of Jo's treachery, it was all I could do to prevent them from beating the shit out of the new boyfriend. But as much as I wanted to see him lying in a bloody pulp, I knew it would only make things worse.

It wasn't long after meeting Mandy when I finally bit the bullet and took my test. It really pissed me off that it was *exactly* the same test as on my Fizzy. It was even the same examiner for crying out loud. It went pretty well except for one slight glitch. After tootling along beside him at walking pace (which the little 200 performed perfectly) I had to switch my engine off while he explained that I was to ride around the same route I'd been using so far, but at some random point he would jump out and hold his hand up. Then I was to perform an emergency stop. I refrained from telling him that I already knew the procedure since I was being obsequiously nice. Didn't want to prejudice his conclusion, don't you know.

"Okay Mr Muir," he said when he'd finished his spiel. "Start your engine and proceed along the course."

And that's when things went wrong. I thumbed the electric start and the motor spun over but nothing happened. I checked that I hadn't accidentally knocked the kill switch and then tried again. Nothing. So I reverted to the kickstart. Still nothing.

"You seem to have a bit of a problem, Mr Muir. Do you know what the cause is?"

Fortunately, I had a fair idea. Tooling around at twenty-eight mph and then pottering along beside the examiner had fouled the plugs. "Yeah," I replied anxiously. "The plugs have fouled."

"I see. Can you fix the trouble?"

"Oh yeah, no problem."

"Good. I'll give you two minutes to sort it out."

*Two minutes? Two flaming minutes?*

In a flash, my seat was up and my toolkit was out. Sure enough, when I took the first plug out, it was black and oily. I didn't have a rag on me, so I used my jeans. As soon as it was clean I replaced it and then made to get the other plug out. But just as I was putting the plug spanner on the plug, I noticed the examiner very deliberately look at his watch. *Sod it, I'll have to try and get it going on one cylinder.*

I thumbed the button and the motor spun for a few seconds before one pot spluttered fitfully to life. Somehow, against all odds I managed to keep it going. Then, *RRRRRUMMMM!* the second pot burst into life accompanied by a huge cloud of choking blue smoke.

"Ahh, that's better," the examiner said calmly. "Shall we proceed?"

It goes without saying that I passed. And that very evening I proudly picked Mandy up from her Judo class. *Up yours, Jo*, I thought bitterly. *You've really missed out on this.*

It was at this point that I reacquainted myself with the Boat Mob. And to my surprise, they welcomed my 200 with as much enthusiasm as they had my 250.

"Yeah, Gary's got one of these," someone said. "It ain't half quick."

And that was pretty much it, meetings-wise. I wasn't going to go there again because I might have run into Jo; and there was no way I could face that! My fall from grace was complete; as far as I was concerned I was a member of the Boat Mob, and was no longer a Jehovah's Witness – for now, anyway.

# 10: THE QUICKEST OF THE QUICK

Being back with my old friends at the Boat felt great. I was with brothers who didn't judge me because my hair was too long or wear the wrong clothes; and they certainly didn't expect me to go knocking on people's doors! My bike liked it as well for I discovered something rather incredible about my RD200. It was quick – no, it was *bloody* quick! At first it didn't really show. Most of the times we went somewhere, Ivor was with us on his little Yamaha YB100, so we kept to his speed. I tell you what though, he could hustle through the lanes at an unbelievable rate of knots on that damned thing. A lot of reasonably good riders on much bigger bikes would have had trouble staying with him.

But if Ivor wasn't present, my bike tended to be the smallest. The others were mostly RD250's. Even so I had no problem keeping up. I once overheard a conversation where it was said that Muir's 200 was unfeasibly quick. My ego puffed up so much it almost didn't fit out the pub door! I was eager to prove it too, but how? A race past the Chef was pointless. The 250's were hitting between ninety-five and a ton, whereas my 200 still hadn't topped eighty-five – and since that was about five hundred revs into the red, it wasn't likely to. So I knew how fast it went, but how quick was it? How well did it accelerate and handle?

Well the handling was becoming pretty clear – it was good. Very good in fact. Probably not quite up to my old RD250 standards, but not far behind. I think the best to be said was that it handled differently to the bigger bike. The 250 swept through the bends and stayed remarkably stable even when cranked over so far that the pegs touched down. And even beyond that since they folded nicely. We used to joke that Smiffy's footrest hangers were so worn that his pegs were in danger of falling off!

The 200's style of cornering was slightly less stable. Rather than sweeping through the bends, it kind of scampered round them like a playful terrier. Even so, it could corner with the best of them, even allowing me to outpace the not-so-bold 250 riders. And talking of bold, nobody could beat Smiffy. Not only was he arguably the best rider, but his bike was obscenely fast for a mere two-fifty. One day I found out why.

It was on a Sunday in mid-to-late May when I popped round his house. I can't remember why, which is odd because I almost never knocked there.

"Is Steve in?" I asked when his dad answered the door.

"Yes, he's in the garage messing around with his bike."

"Is it alright to go through?"

"Of course. No problem."

Except it was a problem. I walked in to see Smiffy sitting on the floor with a file in his hand and one of the bike's barrels between his knees. Someone was with him but I didn't get a chance to see who.

"Get out!" Smiffy shouted, quickly putting the barrel down and leaping to his feet. "*Get out!*" he repeated pointing the file at me threateningly.

I didn't argue. Smiffy was intimidating enough at the best of times. In fact, we sometimes referred to him as O.M.A – One Man Army. Being a very proficient middle weight boxer, his fists were as fast as his bike.

"Sorry," I said, hurriedly backing out. "I just wondered…"

"F\*\*k off!" he shouted.

I turned and left as fast as I could. I wasn't going to argue, but I couldn't help grinning to myself. I now knew his secret. His bike was ported – tuned for more power, and he was opening the ports up even more. Hell that thing was going to *move!*"

A few days later we were in the boat car park, and I saw him eying my bike thoughtfully. As I wandered over, he looked up and fixed me with those piercing eyes of his.

"You want a race?" he asked.

"Not really?" I replied cautiously. "You'll piss all over me past the Chef."

"True. How about from here, into Thong Lane, and up to the A2. We'll stop just before the slip road. See if you can stay on my arse."

There didn't seem a lot of point, considering his renowned skill – especially since he'd given his RD a fair bit more power. But I decided to give it a try anyway. I was pretty good with the clutch, so I might not be embarrassed too badly on pulling away.

We pulled out onto the road and moved away from the pub to where it was safe to line up next to each other.

"On three," Smiffy shouted above the revving of our bikes. "One, two, THREE!"

I slammed the throttle wide open and dropped the clutch – well I fed it in extremely quickly to be more accurate. I threw my weight over the clocks to try and keep the front wheel down. As it was, it lifted off and skimmed along just above the tarmac. I snicked into second gear a fraction of a second later, then into...

"Bloody hell," I muttered in awe. "I'm in front!" And in front I stayed. All the way through the twisties Smiffy was struggling to hang on to me. I was shocked to my very soul. It was the first time I realised exactly how quick my little RD200 really was. It was lightning quick!

A couple of miles later we pulled over. To my amazement, Smiffy leapt off his bike, pulled his lid off and ran angrily up to me.

"I want to see your barrels!" he demanded furiously, thrusting his face into mine.

I was too ecstatic to be scared. I slowly took my helmet off and grinned apologetically. "They're standard," I assured him. "They haven't been touched."

"Bollocks, they can't be!"

"Honest. They've never been off." That wasn't entirely true. I had taken them off once to see if they needed decoking, but other than that I wasn't lying.

"It's impossible. No 200 can be that fast without being tuned."

"Honest..."

"Take it past the Chef," he snapped, stuffing his lid back on and throwing his leg over his bike.

I nodded cautiously; was I going to be embarrassed or had the bike suddenly found a burst of power it had never had before.

I was embarrassed.

I led the way, cranked right over on the tight curve that was the start of the slipway. My pegs were just brushing the tarmac before I straightened up and pulled onto the motorway-styled A road.

For a few seconds, I thought I was going do it. My hopes were quickly shattered, however. When I hit about sixty, Smiffy's blue RD250C flashed past as though I was standing still. Apparently, he topped out a smidge over the ton, and although I'd lain really flat on the tank for the first time, I'd only hit eighty-seven. I'd been well and truly pissed all over. The smirk of relief on Smiffy's face when we got back to the pub was almost as embarrassing as the race. And he couldn't resist telling everyone how he'd destroyed my bike on the A2. A little later, however, I realised my bike had gone faster than ever before. With the rev counter firmly in the red, I'd hit the illusive eighty-seven that the bike mags had promised – even if it was slightly downhill.

Days later my distress was relieved even further when several people told me how incredibly impressed Smiffy had been with my bike. The word was quickly spreading about Muir's amazingly quick 200.

A couple of weeks after that we were sitting in the car park over the rec when we had a visitor. He was a bit of a plonker to be honest, and not deemed fit to join our ranks – especially as he rode a bright yellow Honda CJ250T. For some reason though, I was a little jealous of him. Maybe because he had his girlfriend, Linda, on the back. She had long blonde hair, and... and...

She was *my* girlfriend. Or she had been once. On my first day at school, I'd thought her so pretty that I'd walked straight up to her. And my first words to her? "You're my girlfriend."

And her first words to me? "Okay."

Now here she was on the back of a poxy CJ250!

I mentioned how this bloke was a bit of a plonker. Well he wasted no time before proving the fact. Us being us, we couldn't help but deride his steed.

"I'd rather eat worms than ride a Honda," was the oft repeated saying in the pub. And it was repeated several times that evening, I can tell you.

We all howled with laughter when he declared that his bike was as fast as an RD250.

"It is!" he protested angrily.

"Tell you what," Ivor said with a grin. "Why don't you prove it? See if you can beat Muir's 200 in a drag race."

The plonker's eyes lit up. He must have realised that he was outclassed by the RD250s, but against a little 200? Why not. So a few minutes later we were side by side on the road. From the car park entrance to Vigilant Way – the first road on the right – was a little short of a quarter mile.

It was Jaffa, I believe, who set us off.

"On three. One, two, *three!*"

To say I won is an understatement. Let's face it, from a standing start, even Smiffy's RD250 had no chance.

The red-faced plonker didn't hang around after that. He was gone as soon as he got back to collect Linda. And the big smile she gave me felt almost as good as thrashing the pants off the total idiot and his Honda. Almost.

Not to be outdone, however, he returned a couple of weeks later. But this time he was on a CB550F, complete with the same beautiful blonde as before. He got the same ribbing about his bike though. You know what I mean. "I'd rather eat worms…" etcetera, etcetera.

"At least it'll piss all over your 250's," he said arrogantly.

"Try Muir's 200 again," someone called. To my dismay he agreed. I was going to be crushed, but how could I say no? All I could do was make the race as close as possible.

Once again we lined up. Once again someone gave us the countdown. Once again I let fly, laying on my clocks with the front wheel skimming the tarmac.

And...

Once again, I blew him into the weeds! He was probably just crap at feeding in his clutch, but that mattered not. The legend of Muir's explosive RD200DX had grown even wider and louder. There are many tales about how I proved its legend to be true, and these are but a very few. Some I won't put in print since they're so unbelievable they would elicit howls of "Bullshit!" from all my readers. Suffice it to say that they were all true.

And there's another thing I haven't mentioned about the RD200: the brakes. The earlier drum braked versions had had a bad reputation, stopping-wise. Although not exactly puny, that drum front brake couldn't match the discs that were becoming so prevalent. But the DX version which was mine had a lovely big disk up front. And what with the bike weighing less than an empty shoebox, it could out-brake almost anything you can think of in that era. It was fierce, but it also had plenty of feel. My memory is probably clouded by the passing years, but I reckon it was the best front brake I've ever used.

Another thing I discovered is that the 200 was pretty good off road – tyres and ground clearance notwithstanding.

Ivor, Smiffy, Tony, and I went to a local scrambling track (similar to motocross before motocross was a thing over here) to have a go. We had the place to ourselves, so we really let rip. Ivor's YB100 was probably best suited to the fun and games, but that didn't stop the rest of us from throwing our hats into the ring.

Fortunately, it was a dry day and it was more caked earth than mud. It was still pretty hard going though. Eventually Smiffy, Ivor, and I had had enough of the fun, but as for Tony?

I've never seen a road bike thrown about with such abandon. And his bike soaked it all up, slipping and sliding, bouncing over the bumps far faster than any of the rest of us had dared go. I was somewhat disgruntled to be honest, since the bike he was using and abusing was an RD250B identical to the wicked one I'd owned. I must confess, I felt a pang of regret that I'd swapped it for my 200. Once we were on our way home though, that regret vanished like the morning mist. It was if the 200 was saying, "Don't worry about it; I'm much better than that old thing."

Oh boy did I love that little bike; and just how much was proved to me a week or two after blowing Linda's boyfriend into the weeds.

As readers of *Sixteener Special* will recall, Martin's friend Nigel had a beautiful blue Suzuki T500M. It was a bike I'd lusted after since he'd given me a lift when I was fifteen. One day he pulled up at where a few of us were gathered and informed us that he was selling his bike. My heart leapt at the thought. Could my long held desire to own one of these beasts be about to be realised. Of course my dad would need a lot of persuading, but I was certain I could win him over.

"Are you interested?" Nigel asked, knowing how much I liked it.

"Yeah, very interested," I gushed.

"Take it for a spin if you want."

I very much *did* want.

A few moments later I climbed aboard and ...

"What the..." To my disbelief the handlebars moved. They were rubber mounted which meant that the high and wide bars had a good inch or more movement back and forth. I looked questioningly at Nigel.

"Oh, don't worry, you soon get used to it," he said reassuringly.

I wasn't convinced but I went to start the big 500 up anyway. I reached down with my right hand to push the kick start out (no electric start on this one) but it wasn't there. "Oh yeah," I thought stupidly. "Bloody Suzuki kick starts are on the other side."

I don't know if you've ever tried a left-hand kicker, but they're a bitch to get used to. Doesn't sound as if it should make much difference, but believe me, it does. It took several cack-handed (or cack-*footed*) attempts but eventually it burst into life. And now there was something I *did* like. You could tell it was a two-stroke twin, but the sound was just deeper and somehow more mellow and grown up.

I pulled in the clutch and to my horror, the rev counter stopped working.

"Oh yeah," Nigel said. "The rev counter drive is mounted on the wrong side of the clutch, so it stops turning when you pull the clutch in." I later found out that the oil pump on these bikes stopped at the same time!

Hmmm. I was not amused. But then I pulled away. Wow that big old two-stroke had some torque. And despite redlining at a paltry seven grand or so, it really did fly. All my mates were following me on their 250s, but they had no chance of keeping up. I was intoxicated by its power! A few years later I discovered it had the same performance as the heralded RD400 – the faster E model to boot. As I swept round the first bend in third and then wound the beast up on the straight, I couldn't help uttering my feelings out loud.

"Yuk!"

I hated it. Yes, it went like a scalded cat, but it felt crude and sloppy. My 200 was tight and refined, nimble and well-braked. This thing was like a turbo charged tractor that you might as well drag your heels up the road to try and stop.

Nigel was most disgruntled when I expressed my opinions on our return. It amazed him that I didn't like it. How was it possible? I've asked myself the same question many times over the years. The answer though is simple. My RD200DX really was that good!

## 11: SILVER JUBILEE

1977 was a good year, I suppose. Despite my romantic woes, it was the Queen's Silver Jubilee. As June came the excitement grew, and there was to be a party on the big patch of green that separated one half of my road from the other. Personally, I couldn't give a stuff. In fact, I was now gravitating towards Punk Rock (oh how the JW elders would have despaired) so had recently bought a copy of, "God Save the Queen" by the Sex Pistols. Such disrespect from one so young. At the time I was a confirmed republican, something that has changed over the many years.

One thing that I did like, however, was the fair they were putting on near the River Thames in Gravesend. Yep, I was really looking forward to going to that little shindig. Mandy was coming with us too.

It was late afternoon when the street party started. There was music, all manner of buffet food, and of course, booze. Well the alcohol appeared later in the evening, as did the music, but you get the idea. My contribution to the afternoon's celebrations was erm... unhelpful? I thought it would be a good idea to open my bedroom window and blast my copy of "God Save the Queen" out for the whole street to hear. My father, however, disagreed.

"Turn that racket off," he said in his usual, peculiarly effective, quietly restrained fury.

I always knew I was on dodgy ground when he used that tone, so feigning disappointment rather than fear, I did. Funny how he could terrify me so. In all the years I've been alive, he's never, ever laid a single finger on me. Weird eh?

I went and picked Mandy up at about seven o'clock. We made straight for the fairground where I'd arranged to meet the boys. Smiffy as always was there with his girlfriend, Kim, along with Ivor and many of the gang who I can't remember. I really liked Kim, as we all did, I suppose. Particularly Ivor, since he managed to marry her several years later. But that's another story.

Oddly, I spent very little time with the Boat lot that evening. Many of Mandy's friends were there and it seemed the chivalrous thing to do to join them instead. I was a little concerned at first since Tracy was among them, but she was amazingly forgiving. Okay, she gave me one of her famously foul-mouthed broadsides to begin with, but then we were back to being good friends. She might have had language that would embarrass a sailor, but she really was a great girl.

Mandy, on the other hand, seemed rather remote and low in spirits. Several times I asked her what was wrong but got little in response. At least until I was dropping her off. I went to kiss her goodnight but she kind of pulled away.

"Come on, what's wrong," I asked stroking her hair.

For a moment she didn't answer. Then, "It's Simon. He wants us to get back together."

"What? The way he treated you? He's got a nerve."

"I know but..."

I took a step back in amazement. "You're not thinking about it are you?"

"I don't know... It's just... We were together for so long. I really like you too, so it's difficult."

*Here we go again*, I thought bitterly. "Let me know when you decide," I snapped coldly.

"I..."

I didn't hear the rest, I snatched my spare lid from her, stalked angrily over to the bike, rammed my helmet on, fired the bike up, and screamed it away.

When I got home, the party was in full swing. Once I'd put my helmets indoors, I wandered numbly out to grab a roll or something. The music washed over me unobserved. I stood there watching everyone having fun in solemn self-pity. It was made worse when someone grabbed my arm and spun me around. It was my sister's fiancé, Terry.

"Steve," he slurred, pissed as a newt. "I didn't think you'd be here. Have a drink."

"No, it's okay, Tel. I'm not stopping."

"Shut up," he said, wobbling slightly on his feet. "Here." He pulled me over to the table where the beer was located. He shoved one into my hand and then put his arm around my shoulders. "You and me are gonna be brothers soon. We gotta stick together."

"Brothers in law," I corrected.

"Same fing. You should get married too. Where's that lovely Jo? She was lovely she was. Really lovely."

"She was two-timing me," I said coldly. "She dumped me for another bloke."

Terry shook his drunken head solemnly. "You shouldn't have let that happen. She was a nice girl. Really lovely. You should have brought her here."

"We aren't together anymore Tel. We've split up."

"Yeah, I know. Tell you what, she's really lovely. You should have…"

I managed to get out from under his friendly embrace and smiled at him. "Tell you what, Tel. I'll bring her next time, how about that."

"Yeah, you should. She's really lovely, she is."

I nodded, then managed to get away. I know he meant well, but boy did he turn the knife.

I hadn't heard from Mandy for a couple of days, so one evening I rode over to her house. I didn't quite make it all the way though. I reached the junction opposite the house and there it was: a GT380 parked right outside. Her poxy ex's bike. I stared at it in cold fury for what seemed like forever. I guessed that I'd been dumped again. And possibly two-timed to boot. I switched my bike off and just sat there, watching.

I didn't notice them approach. I was too busy seething to see the two ten-year-old boys until one of them spoke.

"Nice bike," he said cockily.

I sighed and turned my head to look at the pair of them. "Thanks," I replied with weary resignation.

"Not as good as my brother's though," the other lad said proudly.

"Really. What's he got?"

"Yamaha two-fifty," he said in a voice full of challenge.

"Piece of crap," I snorted. "This'll piss all over it."

"F**k off," the first boy in disbelief. "His brother's bike's an RD250. They're the fastest two-fifty on the planet!"

"Yeah," the second boy said proudly. "And anyway, yours is just a stupid little 200."

"Have you ever been on the back of your brother's bike?"

"Of course I have."

"What, even when he's opened it up? I mean, *really* opened it up?"

"Uh-huh."

I chewed my lip thoughtfully. I had my spare lid on my arm just in case Mandy had wanted to go somewhere. So…

"You wanna go on the back of my bike then?"

"Nah. It'll be a slug after my brother's bike."

"What, you scared or something," I said, challenging his pride.

"Go on," the first boy urged. "It's only a 200."

"All right; give us your lid then."

So I did. And when he was safely on board, I fired up the bike. "Hold on tight," I said firmly.

The boy snorted derisively, but even so, he put his arm around my waist and held on tight.

I spun the bike around, took a deep breath, and then let rip. Being two-up always made the front end go even lighter when gunning it from the line, and with the firm grip around my waist, I couldn't lay on the clocks to keep the front wheel near the deck. So I have to say, as we shot away from the line like a bullet from a gun, I pulled a magnificent wheelie.

In retrospect, it was a stupid thing to do. And to make matters even worse, I thrashed the bike mercilessly through the streets. I banked it right over, using the edge of my foot to gauge how close I was to touching the pegs down. Each time I had to brake, I braked as hard and as late I could. If I remember correctly, the whole time my teeth were clenched, and a defiant sneer marred my lips. I was angry and hurt and was taking it out on the little Yam – two-up to boot – but it took it all in its stride.

We arrived back where my poor passenger's friend was waiting. The front tyre howled in protest as I hauled the bike down from light speed to standstill in just a few yards. The poor boy behind me almost fell off the bike when we stopped.

"F***ing hell," he said shakily as he pulled off the crash helmet. His face was as white as chalk and his hands were trembling uncontrollably.

"What's the matter," his friend asked. "Are you okay?"

"That," the lad replied incredulously. "Is the fastest bike I've ever been on!"

"What, faster than your brother's two-fifty?"

"Much faster. It scared the crap out of me." He turned and looked at his friend. "It goes like a f**ing rocket!"

"You wanna go?" I said to his friend.

"Nah, you're all right."

"Go on," his mate said. "It's so quick it'll blow your mind."

His friend shook his head. "Nah, I'll take your word for it."

I shrugged my shoulders. "Fair enough. Give us my lid back then," I said to the poor shaken boy.

Dutifully, he handed it over and stood back to look at the bike. "Thanks mate," he said, his voice full of awe. "That was brilliant."

I smiled. "No problem. And don't forget to tell your brother about it." And with that, I screamed away into the night.

As it turned out, I got a phone call from Mandy the following evening informing me that she was back with Simon. He'd come over the night before to talk to her about it. So that's why his bike was there. I was pretty hurt by her decision, but at least I knew she hadn't two-timed me. Not like that other bitch!

So that was how the Silver Jubilee went for me. I'm guessing most people had a better time of it than I did. Maybe others didn't. But I'm also guessing that not many had a firecracker RD200 to take away their blues; and I have to say, it did a real good job of doing just that.

# 12: SURPRISES GOOD AND BAD

June was an odd month for me in '77. Sad because for the first time in over two years I had no girlfriend, but also joyous because I could now spend all my spare time with my new biker family. And oh what fun we had. Blasting through the lanes, drinking at various pubs (at least the ones that allowed bikers in), racing past the Chef – and even going in there for a coffee and chips. We laughed and messed around, always having fun. I also learned how to use my fists, and to use them well at that. Good job the JW Elders were now firmly in my past.

I can remember one sunny late afternoon leaving my house in a hurry. I can't recall where I was going – it might even have been to pick Mandy up from judo while I was still with her. Wherever it was, I think I was late because I pushed the bike hard from the moment I left home.

Now the Gravesend Boat was not far from my house. Probably about a quarter of a mile. I approached the T junction opposite the pub and took a quick look to my right. The road was clear, so I just opened the bike up and swept around the left turn. As I say, I was pushing hard so I banked the bike all the way over until the side of my plimsoll (which was all several of us wore) touched down. This was usually my warning that I was over far enough. Except I was turning too tight to stop there. My footrest skimmed the tarmac, but then the poxy unhinged peg dug in and threw me off.

It wasn't exactly a bad crash. Although I'd had to crank it over a long way, I was doing twenty mph at the most. In fact, it was probably the most hilarious stack I've ever had. I landed on my arse and while still sitting up, I slid along the road spinning a neat, and rather impressive 360°. The bike did the same alongside me in perfect synchronicity. It really was the most beautiful performance – one which my mates standing in the pub car park really appreciated.

The cheers that erupted were so loud I could hear them above the sound of scraping metal and an over revving engine. The motor cut out just as the pair of us came to rest. Oh the humiliation. There was only one thing to do to cover my embarrassment. I climbed to my feet, and to great applause, I performed a flourishing and theatrical bow. I then picked the bike up, restarted it, and sped away performing a delightfully impressive wheelie. Checking the bike for damage would have to wait until I arrived at my destination. Fortunately, apart from a scuffed footrest rubber and handlebar end, there was really nothing worth mentioning. I did get a free pint for my performance the next time I was in the pub though.

Eventually, June came to a close, and with it came terrible news. Burtons were restructuring and I was to be made redundant. Although I didn't particularly like the job, it was still a crushing blow. Jo had betrayed and dumped me, Mandy had left me for her old boyfriend, and now even my employer didn't want me. The due redundancy pay went a little way toward alleviating the pain though. And yes, I'd suffered worse in my young life – much worse – but I still felt so wretched I could cry.

Things quickly changed in that last week of the month though. Tommy and Allan had booked a holiday at Pontins holiday camp in Blackpool with a couple of other mates. However, one of the party had dropped out.

"Do you want to come?" they asked.

At first, I wasn't sure. Could I afford it? Then it struck me. Of course I could bloody afford it. My redundancy pay would be through any day now.

"Of course I'll come," I said enthusiastically. It would be my first real holiday with no parents watching over me.

Then on the last Wednesday of the month, something else happened. It was my day off and being a lazy sod, I was doing nothing except lay on the sofa reading my old bike mags. To my annoyance I was interrupted by the phone ringing. With a huge sigh, I put my magazine down and hurried out to the front porch where the phone was kept.

"Hello," I said in that familiar questioning voice.

"Hello Steve," came a tentative, female voice. "It's me."

My heart skipped a beat, and all kinds of mixed emotions erupted inside me, the strongest of which was cold and bitter anger.

For a second I was speechless. "Jo," I eventually said icily. "What do you want?"

"Erm... I've got a bit of a problem, and I couldn't think of anyone else who could help me."

"And why would I want to help you?"

"Look, I know how you must feel, but I really do need your help... *please!*"

I let out a deep breath, shaking my head in disbelief. How did she have the nerve to ask me for a favour after what she'd done? Still, I was interested to hear what kind of problem would make her turn to me for help.

"Why, what's the matter?"

"It's rather embarrassing actually. I'm at work and I've split my trousers. I need a lift home so I can change."

"Get you boyfriend to take you," I replied harshly. "You work at the same place after all."

"He's at the other showroom," she said in a strangely awkward voice.

"And?"

"And I can't ask him... We broke up a couple of weeks ago."

"Oh." Once again, my emotions were all mixed up. Along with the anger came a cruel and joyful triumph. "Good," I said harshly.

"Please don't be like that Steve; I really do need your help."

"And what makes you think I can help. I haven't got a full licence," I lied.

"Yes you have. You passed your test about a month ago."

*What the hell?* Was she keeping tabs on me? Martin or Mark must have seen me without L plates and told her.

"Please Steve, I really need your help."

Then, much against my better judgement, I relented. "All right, I'll be there in about twenty minutes. I'll pull up outside the shop."

Twenty minutes later, I did just that. The manageress was watching for me out the shop window while Jo was hiding out the back. Within seconds of me pulling up she came running out. She snatched the spare helmet from my hand and jumped on the back. I had to stifle a laugh as I saw exactly how split her trousers were. From arse to crotch, her knickers were on show for all the world to see.

"Quick," she said, tapping my lid like she used to on my Fizzy. "Let's go."

"I wanted to really scream the bike through the lanes to her house. But the weather was a bit drizzly, so the roads were wet and rather slippery.

I was going to wait outside while she changed but she insisted that I go in with her. The place was just as I remembered it. I plonked myself down in the seat near the fire; the one I'd always sat in. The hearth, however, was unlit and cold. A fitting metaphor, all things considered.

"Would you like a cup of tea?" she asked as she came back downstairs.

"You'll need to get back to the shop, won't you?"

She looked at her watch. "No, it'll be almost my lunch hour by the time we get there."

*Hmm*, I thought sourly. *That's convenient.*

"And anyway, I'd like to have a good talk with you."

"Yeah? What about?"

"Us."

"I didn't think there was an 'us'; you saw to that."

"Please Steve," she said kneeling beside my chair. "You've no idea how sorry I am,"

I looked her in the eyes and sneered bitterly. *Sorry, eh?* I thought. *Well I hope it hurts!*

Of course, the mistake I made was looking her in the eyes. Beautiful eyes that changed colour like human mood stones. They would change from green, to grey, to blue. And today they were blue. Gorgeous blue. The blue that used to make my heart melt. But today I was strong. My heart was as cold as ice, and there was no way she could influence me at all!

I can't remember how long we spent snogging and canoodling. I do know she was late getting back to work though. Her manageress, however, had a knowing twinkle in her eye when I walked Jo into the shop.

"Thanks Steve," she said pecking me on the cheek. "Will you come over tonight? We didn't get a chance to talk, and there really is a lot we need to talk about."

I tried my best to look doubtful, I really did. Let's face it, one snog did not make up for all the pain she'd put me through.

"I'll give you a lift home," I said, all resolve melting like a snowball in a fire.

Her smile of gratitude was like a kick in the stomach – a good kick though, a *nice* kick. It seemed there was a possibility that we would get back together.

All the way home, my 200 buzzed away happily. It sounded as though it was as excited as I was. Even the couple of slides I had were taken in its stride. Even a wet road couldn't dampen our spirits. But my father, whose half-day it was, did his best to do just that.

"You're not really going to pick her up, are you?" he asked in disbelief.

"Yeah. I told her I would."

"You're mad. After the way she treated you? You know she probably planned everything this afternoon."

I shrugged. "I don't see how she split her trousers on purpose. Anyway, I'm only giving her a lift home because she wants to talk."

"She'll wrap you round her little finger. She's always been able to manipulate you." It was a strange reaction considering how much both he and Gwen eventually came to like her.

But no matter how he pressed, I was determined. In the end he let it go with a final, "Oh well, it's your life."

I left home at about ten past five. The skies had cleared a bit, and the roads had dried up. That lovely, creamy-smooth, almost electric wail coming from the twin pipes only added to my excitement. Every bend and corner were a delight as the bike scampered merrily around them. I accidentally lifted the front wheel several times as I pulled out of junctions. I couldn't help but wonder what the evening held. Once or twice it entered my head that my dad was right. I had fleeting thoughts of standing tall and proud, coldly dismissing her tearful pleas. As it turned out, those thoughts were very fleeting indeed.

# 13: DELIGHT AND DISASTER

Jo's family treated my reappearance with a fair amount of suspicion – especially her dad, Colin. As an Elder in the Jehovah's Witness Organisation, there was a possibility that he'd have heard of my recent appalling attendance record. Added to that was the fact that my hair had grown a fair bit since we'd last met – long hair being taboo with the JWs – and my style of dress had got no better. In retrospect he should have thrown me out on my ear, yet despite his obvious dislike for me, he never once tried to keep me away from his precious daughter. We all had a nice cup of tea in the lounge with a not-so-nice feeling of tension in the air. Her brother, Chris, glowered at me, her mother, Joyce, acted with a strained air of politeness, while, as I say, Colin treated me with commendably restrained hostility.

"Dad," Jo said after our tea was drunk. "Steve and I have a lot to talk about. Is it alright if we go up to my bedroom?"

Colin paused for a moment before replying. "Okay," he said carefully. "But leave the door open."

"But dad…"

"I said leave the door open."

"But it's a private chat," she said glaring pointedly at Chris. He did have a habit of eavesdropping on us.

Colin blew out his cheeks while giving me a searching look. "I tell you what," he said at last. "You can sit in the car. But I'm warning you, I'll be watching."

"Thank you," Jo said in that *I knew I'd win* tone I'd come to know so well.

A couple of minutes later we were sitting in the front seats of the family Hillman Hunter which was parked on the road in front of the house. I was behind the wheel which for some reason gave me an unexpected air of confidence.

"So what do want to talk about?" I asked, staring fixedly at the road ahead.

"Us," she replied echoing her previous reply.

"You really want us to get back together?"

"I think we belong together," she said simply.

Somehow, I managed to keep staring straight ahead. I knew it would be disastrous to look at her. I'd only want to start snogging again, which was impossible with Colin on the prowl.

"You didn't think that a couple of months ago." Flipping 'eck. This was like a bad rerun of our previous conversation.

"And I made the biggest mistake of my life. As soon as we broke up I knew I'd made a mistake."

"So how can I trust you? You've destroyed what we had. We were going to be our first and only, now you've screwed someone else, that's gone forever."

"Steve, look at me."

With a deep breath I turned my head and met her eyes. Oops.

"Steve, I swear I never slept with him. Nor the others."

"Others!" I cried in dismay. "What others?" This was going from bad to worse.

"Look," she said taking a deep breath. "I'll tell you everything, and then you'll know you can trust me."

I didn't want to hear it. I just wanted to get out of the car and jump on my bike. At least *that* had never let me down. For some reason though, I stayed and listened. I listened with mounting horror as she spoke of the three men she'd seen in those few short months. And the last one blew me away. He was the company electrician and not only was he about thirty, he was also married.

"Oh come on," I said disbelievingly. "You can't tell me you didn't sleep with *him*. He ain't gonna be content with a quick kiss."

"Honestly, he just gave me a lift home a few times. We kind of just kissed and that was it. And what about you? You must have had another girlfriend in all that time."

"Yeah, two," I said trying not to be outdone. "But to be honest we were more like friends. Nothing happened at all."

And so the conversation went on. Eventually she broke the tension by dropping a bombshell – well kind of.

"You know we're moving next week."

"What? Where to?"

"Oh not far from here. Bean, near Dartford. It's just a few miles through the lanes. We went there to see Roy and Carol, remember? You followed us there on your Fizzy. Dad put us on the council waiting list and we got offered a house almost straight away."

Now in today's overcrowded Britain, to get offered a council house in less than a couple of millennia is almost unheard of, and it usually took a couple of years even back then. But since Jo's house had no hot water, no bathroom, and an outside toilet, the family had been moved to the top of the list.

"Is it a nice house?"

"Me and Chris haven't seen it yet. We're going on Sunday straight from the Meeting. You should come."

Ah, there it was. The invitation to be a part of the family, just like I'd (kind of) been before. But that would entail going to their Kingdom Hall. It would mean acting like a Jehovah's Witness for a day. But although I hadn't missed the Meetings all that much, I had missed my time with Jo and her family.

"Okay," I found myself saying. "I'll come."

Now I know this is beginning to sound like some kind of stupid Mills and Boon romance novel, but there was one very important thing that came out of this conversation. It went like this:

"So, are we back together then?" Jo asked, her blue eyes staring deep into mine.

"I suppose we are. But seriously, it has to be for good."

"It will be. I know now; I don't want anyone else."

"I guess we'll have to get married then," I said light-heartedly.

"Okay, when?"

I paused. Bloody hell, I'd just proposed! "Erm... Well, we're only seventeen, so at least not until we're both eighteen." All at once I was hit by a sudden burst of romantic enthusiasm. My birthday was only a few weeks away, but Jo's? "Next year then, right after your birthday."

"God, no; not in March. I want a June wedding."

"Fair enough then, June it is."

"You'll have to ask dad for my hand," she said with a smile.

Suddenly my enthusiasm disappeared as though a bucket of ice-water had been tipped over my head. Boy did that man terrify me.

"Okay," I said carefully. "When do you think I should speak to him?"

"Right after your birthday."

So as terrifying a thought as the conversation with Colin was, I at least had a few weeks to prepare for the trial. I suddenly remembered my holiday plans with Tommy and Allan at the beginning of August. Fortunately, she was fine with the idea. Who was this girl, and what had she done with my Jo?

So that was that. Everything was sorted. At the tender age of seventeen – and a lazy, irresponsible, prat of a seventeen-year-old at that – my life had been laid out before me in the front (a change from the usual back) seat of a Hillman Hunter.

Although I did tell my dad that Jo and I were now engaged, I kept the actual wedding plans under my hat – at least until I'd spoken to Colin. I got enough of a ribbing from him as it was. And I'd get far more if the big man said no.

"Engaged, eh?" he scoffed "You realise how stupid that sounds. On the same day you get back together you decide to get married." He shook his head in disgust. "You're a pair of children playing at being grownups."

As stinging as his reaction was to my news, I had been prepared for it. It still hurt though.

True to my word, I joined Jo's family at their Kingdom Hall on Sunday. I got a lot of stern looks from members of the congregation, but I didn't care. And nor it seems did Jo's mum and dad. Odd.

Their new house was really nice, and it was big too. I was genuinely pleased for them.

"Shame about this house?" I said to Jo later as we sat alone at the end of her garden. "Nobody will want to rent it, will they. I guess it'll be pulled down or redeveloped. Who owns it?"

"Oh, right," she said with a kind of embarrassed grin. "In a way, I suppose I do."

"What!"

"Yeah. My Uncle Ted owns this one and the empty one next door. He used to live in that one in fact, but he's been in hospital for a few years now. I doubt he'll ever come out, so my dad's been looking after it while Uncle Ted's away. He's leaving this house to me in his will, and he's leaving the one next door to Chris. If he dies before Chris and I are twenty-one, my dad has –

oh what do you call it – authority or whatever it is until we're old enough to inherit."

Now that *was* a surprise.

But enough of the sloppy stuff, back to my true love, the RD200. Obviously things went back to how they'd been before my breakup with Jo. Except of course, I was working out my notice with Burtons and I'd started attending the JW meetings with Jo's family on most Sunday mornings. I wasn't going to go to any of the other meetings though. I was far too busy with my mates. Soon came the time for Jo to become a part of that side of my life.

Everyone up the boat knew about her – how could they not considering they were all prepared to beat the proverbial crap out her interloper of a boyfriend. But the first time any of them saw her was in the Thong Lane car park where we often met up. It was on a Sunday afternoon early in July. A few of the guys were there and she was duly introduced. As I'd expected, she went down a storm. Her bubbly personality, coupled with the way she unconsciously flirted with every bloke she met, saw to that. They were all smitten and I was as pleased as punch.

Not so my bike though. I'm sure the bloody thing was jealous, for when I decided to show off with a blast across the car park, it threw a proper tantrum. Actually, it threw its chain.

I'd just scorched away from the line in the usual blistering take off, when with a crunch and a howl, the back wheel locked up. On inspection it was clear that the chain had come off and had locked itself up twixt cog and swinging arm. I mean *badly* locked up! It took a good twenty minutes to try and free it. Eventually, with many grunts, groans, and greasy hands, it came free. The damage to it was startling. Three of its links were badly twisted, giving the chain a rather alarming kink which gave off a loud crunch every time that part of the chain went around the cogs. Ouch!

The cause of the mishap was obvious: the rear wheel was loose. The spindle nut hadn't been tightened when the chain had been adjusted – except it had. I knew it had. I'd adjusted it over a week ago and had done a good hundred miles or so in the meantime. A fair few of them with Jo on the back. Suspicion would naturally fall on someone in the car park loosening it. But firstly, none of my mates would do such a thing, and secondly, nobody had been near the bike. They'd all been too busy being charmed by Jo! So how the hell had it happened other than the bike being jealous? I look forward to any suggestions from my readers.

Clearly, the chain needed replacing as soon as possible, which given my usual can't be arsed attitude, wasn't anytime soon. I did, however, ride with uncharacteristic caution until I could get round to laying out for a new one.

Disaster came when out with my mates the very next Saturday. Yes, Saturday. I'd finished my notice at Burtons the day before, so at last I could join the weekend revelry with the Boat Mob. We were in the pub when it was decided that there would be a race past the Chef. Since my chain was knackered and there was no point in my 200 racing against the 250s anyway, I decided to wait for them all at the turnoff which marked the end of the race. I sat in the lorry park there waiting for them to arrive with Ivor and his YB100.

"Give us a go," he said nodding to my bike.

"No chance," I replied firmly. "The chain's buggered, remember?"

"That's okay; I'll be careful."

"Oh yeah, of course you will," I replied with heavy sarcasm.

Ivor was impervious to my scorn. "Come on, give us a go," he repeated.

"No."

"Oh, go on."

"No!"

Eventually, however, he wore me down. "Oh alright then," I said with heavy resignation. "But be careful!"

"Of course I will."

And off he went. I waited for what seemed an eternity for him to arrive back, but he didn't. Soon the other guys arrived having finished their pointless race – pointless because everyone knew that Smiffy's bike would win. But still no Ivor. Eventually a search party was mounted with me on the back of Tony's RD250B. Had Ivor crashed? Was he lying injured under a car? Or even worse, had he damaged my bike?

As it turned out, it didn't take long for the answer to become clear. Not far away we found him standing forlornly beside my stranded 200. I don't know whether he'd been thrashing it off the line, had tried a wheelie, or if the chain had just eventually given up, but there it was, finally snapped. I was incandescent with rage. I shouted into Ivor's face, accusing him of ignoring my order to take it easy. He in turn, angrily insisted that he had.

Smiffy was a hero that day. "Whatever happened it's done," he said calmy pushing us apart. "I've got a couple of spare chain links at home. I'm pretty sure they're the same size so it'll only take a jiffy to fix. I'll be back in a minute."

He screamed away, and soon after, everyone else left as well. Ivor got a lift back to his YB100 leaving me there all alone. Smiffy, though, was back in less than ten minutes. He was armed with a chain splitter and some spare split links. In no time at all, the chain was in better nick than before.

"There you go, all done," he said getting to his feet and wiping his hands on the rag he'd thoughtfully brought with him. "Let's go and get a pint to celebrate."

His wry wit drew only a scowl, but even so, I was delighted the chain was fixed. And who cared if it now had three split links. It no longer had that terrible twist and ran as smooth as it ever had. For a couple of hundred yards, anyway.

With a terrible thud accompanied by the screech of a locked rear wheel, I came to a stop. At first I thought the chain had come off again, locking the back wheel like it had before. But to my horror, I had no such luck. You see, the RD200's gearbox layshaft is held in place by a horseshoe shaped spacer beside the front sprocket. The spacer is held in place by a plastic – yes plastic – cover. When the chain had snapped it had smashed the cover allowing the spacer to drop off, which then allowed the layshaft to move which in turn had locked the gearbox up completely.

My wonderful, beloved, fantastic RD200DX was buggered – terminally unless it had some serious and prohibitively expensive surgery.

What the hell was I going to do?

# 14: SURGERY AND A NEW BEGINNING

Getting the bike back home had proved relatively easy. Smiffy went off and found a bit of rope to tow it back to my house, and by removing my chain we were able to bypass the totally locked up gearbox. I stood in dazed incomprehension while Smiffy undid the rope. For the first time in almost two years, I was without a bike – well a working one, anyway. I felt as though a part of my soul had been ripped away.

There was nothing for it but to drown my sorrows in a pint of beer. So once the bike had been stowed in the back of the garage, I climbed morosely onto the back of Smiffy's 250 and went to the Boat.

News of the tragedy was greeted with the kind of empathetic sorrow that would normally accompany the death of a friend's close relative. The general opinion was that it was beyond economical repair and should be broken up for parts. This of course only served to increase my feelings of despair.

Then on Sunday afternoon came a ray of hope – albeit a slim one – in the form of Baz.

Baz was a strange individual and was often the target of (mostly) good-natured piss taking. For a start he was from the other side of the Atlantic. He got really peeved when referred to as a Yank, vehemently insisting that he was Canadian. So obviously we never avoided the opportunity to call him a Yankie. It was just such fun. One thing to note about Baz is that I once let him take my 200 past the Chef. On return he jumped up and down with excitement. He'd insisted that with the rev counter showing 10,000 rpm – a full grand into the red – he'd got ninety out of it. An amazing top speed marred only by the small fact that he was well known to...well...um...*stretch* the truth.

The point is that, amid all the doom and gloom, he piped up and said, "I can fix it."

His declaration was met with an unfair level of scepticism, but since I knew him to be mechanically competent, I grasped his offer of help with both hands, and feet, and teeth. This guy definitely knew his way around an engine. His bike, after all, was a bastard RD350 that he'd cobbled together and had tuned himself. It was very much a Frankenstein's Monster, but more of that later.

So with hope in my heart, we arranged for him to come round to my house first thing in the morning. He said he'd be there at nine o'clock, but once again he stretched the truth, leaving me standing there beside my bike for what was an eternity of frantic anxiety. The lying sod didn't turn up until at least five-past. A whole three hundred nail-biting seconds late!

First he examined the bike. He put the chain back on to try and coax the recalcitrant gears to disengage. He clicked his tongue thoughtfully when the damned thing refused to play along.

"We'll have to split the engine," he declared decisively. "Have you got some tools."

"Yeah, I've got the bike's toolkit and some Stillsons. I've got a couple of other bits too."

Baz raised an eyebrow. "What about a socket set?"

I shook my head.

"Huh," he snorted. "So I suppose an impact driver is out of the question?"

Since I had no idea what an impact driver was, I could only shake my head again.

"Okay, I'll have to go and see what I can do. I'll be back in a minute."

He mounted his 350 and kicked the raucous, vicious-sounding engine into life.

"Ding's got a decent socket set," he shouted above the noisy motor. "And I've got some stuff that should help." He shot away from my garage making a hell of a din. Boy did it sound odd. Good but odd. Not like any RD I'd heard before, or since come to that.

I sat down beside my stricken bike to await his return. This time it really was a long wait. It was a full hour before he returned. But the wait was worthwhile, for when he came back, he had a large carrier bag full of tools carefully balanced in his lap.

It only took an hour or so to get the motor out and the head and barrels off. Then came the part that stumped us both.

"Have you got a Hayne's Manual?" he asked in a way that suggested he knew the answer.

"I didn't think I'd need one for a brand-new bike."

"Always get a Hayne's," he said sagely. "Whatever bike you've got." Good advice, and something I've done ever since. "Come on, I'll take you to Halfords. They're bound to have one."

It was the first time I'd been on the back of his bike. To be honest, I'd never been impressed with it. It had started life as a 1973 green RD350. His older brother had owned it but when he'd moved away, he'd left it to Baz who, not having a full licence, had converted to a 250. Unwilling to look out of place on such an 'old' bike, Baz had got hold of the same bronze RD250B tank, side panel, and oil tank that I'd had on mine. He'd also fitted a very racy looking Two-Four seat. After a while he'd decided to make it a 350 again. Unfortunately, he could only lay his hands on the earlier YR5 barrels and pistons. These fitted nicely, but dissatisfied with that, he'd had a go at porting it. And as for the racket it made, cut down baffles and open bell mouths on the carbs saw to that. He also removed the 250 decals from the side panels but never did replace them with 350 ones.

As I say, although it was very fast, I'd never been particularly impressed. But that ride into Gravesend changed all that. It not only went well, but the sound it made when it hit the power band was spine tingling. From onboard it sounded like an angry Ferrari! I was now in awe of the Bastardised beast of a machine.

An hour or so later we were back to my bike, armed with the much-needed Hayne's manual. Baz was pretty good with the spanners. And his knowledge about engines far surpassed my own. Even so, the motor didn't want to play ball. Everything went fairly well until it came to splitting the crankcase halves. Before pulling them apart, we needed to get the alternator off the end of the crankshaft.

"We really need a puller to get this off," Baz said with a grin. "But there's a neat trick to do it without one."

I didn't know what a puller was, and I couldn't quite see what he did, but it looked like he screwed an engine bolt or something into the alternator until it popped off. A neat trick indeed.

Now unlike the 250 and 350 Yams, the RD200 (and the 125) had a vertically split crankcase instead of the easier horizontal split. And instead of good sturdy bolts, the 200's were held in place by bloody Phillips screws, which like all Jap bikes of the period were made of bloody plasticine! Still, the impact driver took care of most of them – all except one which was too far recessed to get the magic impact driver on. We tried an ordinary screwdriver but that only managed to bugger up the screw's head. So once again, I felt despair rising up to strangle my heart.

"Hmm," Baz said thoughtfully. "I guess we'll have to get brutal."

I watched in amazement as he got out a large sturdy flathead screwdriver. I couldn't help wondering how this was going to help. But with the aid of a heavy hammer, he used the flathead to cut a slot into the damaged screw head which was enough for the flathead to get a good purchase on it. Then with me pushing hard against the other side of the motor and

Baz straining against the screwdriver, the screw finally shifted. Success.

Getting the engine to split was a real swine of a job. The halves just wouldn't budge. We kept whacking it with the rubber end of the hammer but to no avail. Checking the screws we'd removed against the Hayne's manual proved that everything had been undone with nothing left to hold the halves together. In the end we gave up and decided to leave it until the morning. On the one hand I was disappointed, but on the other, it was gratifying to see just how far we'd got.

The next morning, Baz came round again, this time armed with a solid looking piece of wood. Using that as a drift, we hammered away, fiercely pounding on the slowly splintering piece of wood. We even used a screwdriver to try and prise the halves apart (not something I'd recommend). Eventually a gap began to appear as the motor finally gave up the fight. At last the halves were separated and we got a glimpse of the damage the gearbox had suffered.

"F***ing hell," Baz said in amazement. "I've never seen anything like that before."

And even I could see why. The layshaft had twisted and bent, while the dogs on several of the cogs were completely stripped.

"Well there's no way to repair that," Baz said with a finality that kicked me in the gut.

"So what am I going to do?" I asked in a choked voice. "Am I going to have to scrap it?"

"Nah, we'll just go to the breakers and see if they've got a 200 layshaft. They'll probably have some cogs in stock too. We'll take a trip up there tomorrow, okay?"

"Okay," I replied trying not to sound too upset. "Where is the breakers anyway?"

"Forest Hill. There's one at Greenwich too, but I think Forest Hill is more likely to have the parts we need."

I nodded. I had hoped that maybe I could get there without him, but it was far too late to ask Gwen to give me a lift. And anyway, I didn't really know what I needed.

The wait was awful. My stomach felt as if it was more twisted than the buggered layshaft. Added to that, I couldn't go and see Jo. When I spoke to her on the phone, I didn't quite get the sympathy I'd hoped for – or needed. Although she didn't say as much, I could sense the anger in her voice. I'd buggered up my bike which she thought was going to affect her life as much as mine – as if.

The next day arrived but Baz didn't. By lunchtime I could take it no longer, so I put all the parts of the broken gearbox into a bag and walked round to his house. There I found him in his shed doing something dubious to what was obviously a partially stripped RD engine.

"I thought you were going to take me to the breakers," I said unsuccessfully trying to hide my frustrated anger.

"Oh yeah, sorry about that, but this RD250 engine came up and I have to... um... see to it quick. I'll be with you in a minute."

From behind I couldn't see what he was doing, but from his movements it looked as though he was filing something on the engine. It took a fair bit longer than a minute, but eventually he was finished. He hurriedly covered the engine with a blanket, and then we were on our way.

I was really impressed with his bike. Although there was a pronounced powerband, it felt as though the bottom end had a nice spread of torque as well. I was even more impressed when we hit the A2. It effortlessly surged up to a good eighty plus with nary a hint of vibration. Very sophisticated – apart from the wonderful, if a little raucous, music from the engine. Hell, I could even hear it at this speed! Strangely enough, when I got to ride it, I found it quieter in the pilot's seat. Perhaps the tailwind on that journey had allowed the racket to reach my ears. Who knows.

The London traffic was a breeze. I was sure I was right about the bottom end. Even out of the generous powerband it had enough performance to easily sweep past anything we met. It certainly was a torquey motor. The only thing I noticed was that Baz tended to miss the occasional gear.

The breakers was huge – to my inexperienced eyes anyway. We walked in to see many damaged bikes, which were presumably waiting to be stripped. Behind a counter I could see rows and rows of shelves holding all manner of parts. Tanks, wheels, whole engines, and what were obviously the innards of others.

Baz walked confidently up to the counter and rang a bell, just like the ones you get in a hotel. A short while later a burly guy in dirty overalls appeared from between the shelves of mechanical goodies.

"What can I do for you?" he asked with just the trace of an impatient smile.

"We need a layshaft and some cogs for an RD200," Baz said in his cheerful transatlantic accent. "We need the layshaft spacer and cover too."

"Uh-huh. Which model?"

"A '76 DX."

The man rubbed his chin thoughtfully. "Hmmm... No, I'm pretty sure we don't have one of those. Might have an earlier model though."

"That might do," Baz said nodding his head sagely. "If you have, can we see it? We've brought the original parts to compare."

"Yeah, no problem." He turned and hesitated for a moment as if trying to recall where the wanted part might be hiding. He then disappeared out the back with a confidence-inspiring stride.

"Will an older gearbox fit?" I asked.

Baz shrugged. "Should do but I guess we'll see."

A short while later the man returned with some parts in a plastic basket. "There you go," he said placing the basket on the counter and taking out the parts he'd found. "That should fit."

Baz took my damaged parts from the bag and carefully compared them with the new ones. To my eyes they looked completely different, but after a moment or two Baz nodded. "Yep, that should do the job. How much?"

The man gave us the price which thankfully was less than I'd feared. I duly handed over the money and we left the shop.

"Are you sure it'll all fit? I asked as we got back to the bike.

"I can't see why not. Dimensions are the same and your selector drum fits the forks perfectly."

"But the cogs look a different size."

"I wouldn't worry about that. As long as the shafts and drum fit okay, we can worry about the gearing later."

I had no idea what he was on about, but he seemed confident enough, so my fears were somewhat alleviated.

When we got back to my garage Baz married the shafts up to each of the crankcase halves in turn. "There you go," he said cheerfully. "Fits a treat."

"Brilliant," I said, my face flushed with relief. "Let's start getting it all back together."

"Sorry Steve; I've got to disappear for a few days. You can wait for me to get back or you can rebuild it yourself."

My stomach dropped to my boots. "I don't think I can put it back together without your help."

"Sure you can," Baz breezed. "The parts are all laid out in order, and you've got the manual. It's a piece of cake."

I took a deep breath and looked at the complicated jigsaw puzzle at my feet. "You really reckon I can do it?"

"Without a doubt. I'll even leave my tools with you, if you want."

I nodded dumbly. I was overwhelmed by the complexity of the task, but nonetheless I resolved to give it a try. After all, the Haynes Manual was pretty clear on the process, and if I followed the instructions carefully, what could possibly go wrong? Two days later I was to discover the answer to that question.

I was so proud of myself when everything was back together. Although singlehandedly getting the motor back into the frame had been a struggle, the only thing I could see wrong were the badly routed breather and overflow pipes. Nothing to worry about though. In my head I went through everything I'd done to the engine and nodded confidently. Yes, I was sure everything was where it should be, and all the nuts and bolts were properly tightened.

Then came the moment of truth.

With my heart pounding anxiously I turned the key.

Good. Nothing blew up and the neutral light glowed reassuringly bright. Trembling with anticipation, I pushed the choke lever down and pressed the starter button. The motor whirred for a few seconds before bursting into life. I'd done it!

I picked up my crash helmet and excitedly jammed it on my head. With a huge grin on my face, I stamped it into first gear and pulled away. Everything seemed fine and dandy. My relief knew no bounds. Treating it gently at first, I headed for the A2 to give it a bit of a run. That was when the first problem reared its ugly head. The gearing was way out. Nine thousand rpm used to equate to eighty-one mph but now made just over seventy-five. Never mind, I thought, Baz said something about seeing to the gearing. He'll sort it when he gets back.

Then I noticed the killer blow. I was leaving a long straight trail of white smoke in my wake. Something was definitely wrong somewhere.

I did nothing more to the bike after that. The coming weekend was an important one, for my sister was getting married the very next day.

\* \* \*

It was a lovely wedding. The sun was shining in a beautifully clear blue sky, and my sister looked radiant. Everything went off without a hitch and even better, Gwen did me a huge favour by fetching Jo to bring her to the reception. Perfect. The only cloud on the horizon was the anxiety gnawing away at the back of my mind. I was certain that I'd screwed up putting the bike back together. I couldn't wait for Baz to get back, which he didn't do for another whole week.

The following Saturday morning he bowled into the pub with a big grin on his face. Wherever he'd been and whatever he'd been doing had obviously gone well.

"I see you fixed your bike," he said cheerfully.

"Kind of," I replied sheepishly.

"What do you mean, kind of? It's standing outside."

"Well it runs okay, but the gearings too low and it's smoking out the left-hand pipe."

He frowned. "Hmmm... Well I expected the gearing to be out and that's easily sorted, but as for the smoke? I'd better come and have a look."

We went outside and I fired up the bike. Sure enough, white smoke poured out of the left-hand exhaust.

"Aw, crap." Baz said with a groan. You've f***ed up the left-hand crank seal. How the hell did you do that?"

Since I was only vaguely aware of what a crank seal was, I had no idea what I could have done wrong. "I don't know," I said morosely. "Can you fix it?"

"Oh yeah," Baz snorted sarcastically. "All we've got to do is strip the motor right down again. We're right back to square one. You've really buggered it up."

"Oh for crying out loud," I said despairingly. "Not again. I'm bloody sick of this f***ing bike." And I was. Gone was all the pride and joy of owning the quickest 200 in town. I found myself wishing with all my heart that I'd bought the Honda instead.

Baz gave me a strange look. "Really?" he asked curiously. "You hate it?"

"F***ing right I do." It was unusual for me to swear so profoundly at that time in my life, so it was definitely apparent that I really did hate the damned thing.

"Do you wanna swap?"

"What do you mean, swap?" I asked, somewhat confused.

"Just what I say. A straight swap; your 200 for my 350."

My mouth opened and closed a few times as his offer gradually sank in. I turned and looked at his bike. Apart from the Two-Four seat it looked identical to my old wicked RD250B – unless you noticed the carbs that was. And it wasn't as shiny of course, but then it wouldn't be, would it.

"Are you serious?" I asked, baffled at the odd suggestion.

"Yeah, I'm serious. Do you want it?"

I looked at his 350, then at my 200, then back at his 350. *An actual 350* I thought in wonder. Something that couldn't be ridden on L plates. I would be on a level way above my mates, and the thing was far faster than anything I'd owned to date. It was also one of the few bikes that could stay with my 200 off the line, and would then storm away from about thirty mph upwards – and I mean storm!

But then again it was a loud, uncouth, bastardised machine that looked as though it was only a 250. Who in their right mind would make such a stupid deal?

"You're on," I said with a huge grin.

So the deal was struck, the swap was made, and by the end of the day, I was the proud owner of an RD350/A/B/YR5 or whatever else it was. But whatever it was, it was mine. Yes, it had its little foibles, but it went like stink. I was as pleased as punch, and so, surprisingly, was Jo.

My eventful second year on two wheels had come to a close with hope and success.

But my eighteenth birthday had been a few days ago, so now I had to face Jo's dad. The thought of that terrified me more than anything in my life!

# 15: A TERRIFYING CONVERSATION

It was the last Sunday in in July; a fitting analogy since it felt as though it could be the last day of my life. I was unsure of how Colin was going to react, but murder was certainly one possibility.

I rather enjoyed pulling into the Dartford Kingdom Hall's car park. To my rebellious heart, the disgusted looks I got from those about to enter the place was a joy to behold. My new bike looked almost as wicked as it sounded. Well maybe not; nothing could look as evil as the way the motor in this vicious beastie sounded! It seemed odd to be wearing a suit and tie while riding such an animal though, but this was the required dress code at the Kingdom Hall, and I was determined to impress the man who was (possibly) to be my future father-in-law.

To say I was nervous is perhaps the greatest understatement in the history of humankind; I was petrified. But I was relieved to see that Jo and her family were already there, and even more so to see that she'd saved me a seat. She smiled warmly as I walked over and sat down. Colin regarded me cooly but still gave me a barely perceptible nod of greeting.

It must be said that although I now avoided all the weekly Meetings, I had occasionally enjoyed the forty-five-minute talks which were the first half of the Sunday gathering. They were sometimes informative and would occasionally challenge my knowledge of the Bible – which wasn't as good as it was supposed to be. Most of the time though, they were as boring as hell. What kind of talk this one was, however, I had no idea. I was far too preoccupied, rehearsing what I was going to say to Colin. I fidgeted and wriggled in my seat, drawing an occasional stern look from him, and a firm dig in the ribs from Jo.

When the two-hour slog came to an end, a couple of Jo's friends came over to chat with us. One of them was Elaine, who had been her best friend for many years now. I didn't particularly like her for one very good reason: she hated my guts and had often tried to persuade Jo to dump me. I had a sneaking suspicion that she'd had a hand in our recent breakup as well. Although today she tried to hide her derision, I could feel the tension and her disappointment that I was back on the scene. This didn't exactly soothe my nerves, and I was hugely relieved when Jo's brother came over to inform us that we were leaving.

It was a dismal ride as I followed them back to their new house. Although the bike sounded good enough in the mid-range and fantastic when it came on song – even at tick-over it sounded mean – at low revs it sounded horrible. It was an awful, deep and mournful dirge which seemed to echo my mood exactly. I was sure I was in for trouble.

The afternoon was unbearable. After being shown around their really nice new house, Jo's mum, Joyce, cooked dinner, while the rest of us sat watching telly. At least they did. My attention was wandering all over the place. As time passed so my anxiety grew. And for a good reason. Colin was a strict Jehovah's Witness and was an Elder in the congregation. According to the Watchtower rules, whatever his children did reflected on him. So if Jo or Chris went astray in some way or another, he could be relieved of his Elder's responsibilities and demoted. Yes, it is a terrible and controlling cult. It was generally accepted that were Jo to marry, it would be in her twenties and the groom would be an obedient and devoted Jehovah's Witness.

I on the other hand was barely eighteen while she was almost a year younger. But worse than that, I had only the most tenuous grasp on the religion's many responsibilities and had recently turned my back on the whole Organisation. Colin was going to flip when I finally plucked up the courage to broach the subject.

As usual, dinner was delicious. Apart from her habit of overcooking the vegetables, Joyce was a good cook. This was just as well because if something wasn't cooked to Colin's high expectations, he would criticise her offering with savage cruelty. To be frank, he was a bully. And I knew that at some time in the distant past, he'd been a violent arsehole. So as the empty plates were taken to the kitchen, I took the opportunity to escape his presence and help with the washing up.

"Are you okay?" Jo whispered as we both dried the dishes.

"Yeah, I'm fine," I lied.

She gave me one of her looks. She knew me too well to deceive her like that. "When are you going to speak to him?" she asked quietly.

"Later on," I replied.

"When?"

"Later."

"Do it now," she urged.

"We're doing the dishes," I hissed back.

"As soon as we've finished them then."

Swallowing hard, I nodded. Of all the times I'd almost stacked my bike, nothing had caused such terror in my guts. I dearly wanted to turn and run, and only Jo's presence kept me from doing just that.

When we were all back in the lounge and everyone was watching telly, I prepared myself to speak up. Yes, I was ready. In just a few moments I would speak. Just a few moments... then just another few moments. Several times Jo dug me in the ribs, and I could swear colin spotted it and had smirked slightly. But no matter how I procrastinated, eventually I could put it off no longer.

"Colin," I began cautiously. "Can I have a word?"

"Ah," he said giving me a piercing look. "I've been waiting for this all day. Right, everyone out of the room," he commanded firmly. I started to comply but suddenly realised he couldn't have meant me. I would have gone red with embarrassment had my cheeks not already been burning brightly. I was sweating like a pig as well.

Once everyone had gone, he fixed his overbearing gaze on me, and stared deep into my eyes. "So, what do you want to talk to me about?"

"Well... erm... I was kind of wondering... um... if... you know... um..."

Was it my imagination or was he really hiding a big smirk behind those intimidating features?

"Well?" he urged. "Out with it."

Somehow, I managed to pull myself together. "I want to ask for Jo's hand in marriage," I blurted out.

"I see," he said sternly, sitting back in his chair. "Are you both serious about this?"

I nodded dumbly.

"Hmmm," he murmured thoughtfully. "Don't you think you're both far too young?"

I took a deep breath. I was clearly going to have to persuade him, but at least he hadn't killed me – yet. "Yes, we are young, but we love each other and we want to marry as soon as we can."

"I see. You really are sure – I mean absolutely certain?"

"Yes, we are."

"Both of you?"

I nodded emphatically.

For what seemed like an eternity he silently searched my eyes.

"Very well," he said at last. "But there are conditions before I agree. First of all, you've been skipping a lot of meetings lately, haven't you?"

How the hell did he know that? He must have been keeping tabs on me after all.

"Yeah, I suppose I have missed a few."

The incredulous look he gave me proved he knew it was more than just a few. "Hmmm. Well if you want to marry her you're going to have to do better than that. You're going to have to go to *all* the meetings from now on."

"Yeah sure," I replied, my stomach sinking. That was really going to damage my social life.

He chewed his lip thoughtfully. "In fact, you can come to all to our meetings here at Dartford instead of just Sunday." He suddenly grinned. "That way I can keep an eye on you."

I frowned slightly. What was going on? How was this going so well? "That's fair enough."

"Okay, I give you my permission."

My jaw dropped into my lap. Had I heard right? Had this ogre been a pussy cat all along?

"There is one more thing though," he added even more seriously than before.

*Here we go*, I thought. *Now comes the big problem.*

"What's that, Colin?"

"Before you go ahead, I want you to know this: she's a cow, she's a bitch, she's manipulative, she's as stubborn as mule, and she'll make your whole life a misery."

My eyes widened in surprise. I would never have expected to hear that from her own father.

"Now, knowing that, if you want to walk away, that's fine by me. But if you do get engaged, you *will* marry her. If you pull out, I'll cross the world to track you down, and when I find you, I'll kill you."

I was shocked. He was supposed to be a devout 'Christian'. Surely he was exaggerating. But by the look in his eyes, I could tell he was deadly serious.

"Do you understand?"

I nodded. I very much understood.

"Okay then, ask me again."

"Sorry?"

"I want you to ask me again."

"Erm, Colin, can I have your permission to marry Jo?"

His face suddenly lit up with a grin so huge it threatened to split his cheeks. "Of course you can," he said with a merry laugh. "Come on you lot," he called loudly. "You can come back in now."

By the way the three of them almost fell through the door, it was clear they'd been trying to listen to what was being said.

"Steve's asked for Jo's hand in marriage, and I've agreed," Colin explained formally.

"Wonderful!" Joyce gushed happily, while Jo ran over to her dad and gave him a big hug.

"Thank you, dad, thank you," she said, overjoyed.

"All right, all right," he chuckled from beneath her tight embrace. "Go and sit down, we've got serious things to discuss."

Obediently Jo disentangled herself and came and snuggled up next to me on the sofa – something she'd never been able to do in front of the family before. And Coin didn't react. Even when I put my arm around her, he said nothing. It was obvious that the family dynamic had changed completely.

"What do want to talk about, dad," Jo asked happily.

"First, your engagement. As far as I'm concerned, you are engaged, but I want it to be kept quiet until after your birthday Jo. I don't want to have to fight the other Elders over this. Once you're eighteen, they can take a running jump, but until then, it could cause trouble."

"But dad," Jo complained loudly. "If we're engaged, we're engaged!"

"Sorry, but that's one of the conditions I'm making. Take it or leave it. I don't want to see a ring on your finger until then, understood?"

"Okay," Jo said with a deep sigh. But I knew what she was thinking. Colin might not want to *see* a ring on her finger, and she couldn't wear one at the Kingdom Hall, but nothing was going to stop her wearing one at any other time. Hell, I suddenly realised I was going to have to buy one. My redundancy money was being quickly whittled away. There was my upcoming holiday and now a bloody ring.

"Right then," Colin continued." I don't want you to have a long engagement, that wouldn't look good, so when are you planning to have the wedding?"

"June the third," Jo replied firmly.

"*June?* Colin cried. "So soon?"

"Well," I replied. "You said you didn't want us to have a long engagement." I was rather surprised by my own courage.

"I know, but June? That doesn't give us long to make all the plans. It's only three months after your birthday."

"But it's a whole ten months from now, Colin."

He seemed to deflate into his chair. "June," he muttered quietly. He suddenly perked up and grinned mischievously. "Where are you planning to live?"

"We hadn't really thought about it," I said with a slight shrug.

"Well I have," he said with a wicked chuckle. "I've always known you were going to ask to get married."

Bloody hell. No wonder he'd been smirking all day. He'd known we'd want to get married even before *we* did. It also explained why he'd broken JW protocol all this time, and even though he'd appeared to hate me, had allowed me to be kind of part of the family. And my squirming would have made it obvious that today was the day I was going to ask. Smug bastard!

"I couldn't think where you would live, but now that we've moved, I think you should live in our old house, Jo."

It was the perfect solution. It was virtually Jo's house anyway. My future father-in-law was a genius. So from then on, we began to decorate and make repairs to the place that would eventually become our home. Married at eighteen, eh? What a pair of idiots.

And as for keeping the engagement a secret, I was right. There was no way Jo was going to do that. So I bought her an extremely nice (and very expensive) eighteen carat diamond and sapphire ring that she chose. And she only took it off when at home or at the Meetings. Even a couple of her JW friends were in on the secret. It seemed they were really happy for us both, but nothing could prepare us for the way the Boat Mob reacted.

The Saturday evening when we announced the engagement in the pub, we were met with a riotous chorus of congratulations. Jo was now a welcome member of our crowd, which gave us both a weird kind of double life. Some days we were good little Jehovah's Witnesses who wouldn't say boo to a goose, while at other times we were part of a crowd of rebellious bikers.

Oh how strange our lives had become. And indeed, the next year would prove to be the weirdest year of my life so far. But that's another story altogether, and one that deserves a book of its own. Book three in this series should be a riot.

# 16: WHY SO QUICK?

At the time of writing, it has been forty-seven years since the demise of my RD200. I can proudly say that I've been a biker all my life – even when I lost my licence through illness, I continued my relationship with bikes by rebuilding an old and rusted heap. It's no bullshit when I say that I've owned or used some sixty-odd bikes in my time, from a little Puch VS50D moped, to a big black Mk1 Triumph Speed Triple. I've covered almost five hundred thousand miles in that time, most of them as a despatch rider. But of all the bikes I've ever owned, used, or hired, that little 200 is one of my favourites. Every time I think of it I smile, and I've never stopped wondering why it was so quick.

Three years after I swapped it, I had the opportunity to get my hands on another one. In a strange parody of before, I swapped my GT500 Suzuki for it. This 200 was identical to my old one, apart from one small thing that is – it was a slug!

Actually, that's not strictly true. It was significantly quicker than my friend's GT185, but there was no way it would out accelerate an RD250, let alone a CB550F! It was, I suppose, just a common or garden RD200. Very fast for the 200 class, but not supernaturally quick like mine had been.

So why the hell *was* it so quick?

After a few decades of pondering on it, I've come up with two, or perhaps three explanations.

The first is the way I ran it in. My careful and fastidious process has proved beneficial in other bikes I've owned. Years later, the despatch company I rode for bought a batch of Honda VT500s. Although they were company bikes which we had to rent, after eighteen months, they would become the property of the rider. So since I would one day own the bike, I performed my usual, ridiculously careful running in procedure.

Not long after running it in though, some prat pulled straight out in front of me, writing off my precious 500. However, one of the other VT500 riders had left the company the day before, so I was offered his bike instead. It had only done a couple of hundred miles more than mine, but it had been thrashed mercilessly from day one, and was frankly awful. It felt rough and sluggish in comparison. I turned the bike down there and then. I've also owned a GSX400EZ Suzuki which the previous owner had, to all intents and purposes, run in for an incredible ten thousand miles! And that beast was also faster than it had any right to be. But neither of these examples were so much quicker than other identical models the way my 200 had been.

The second idea I had was the gearing. All the tests I've ever read put the top speed of the RD200 between eighty-five and eighty-seven, whereas mine hit the redline at a mere eighty-one. Since it hit peak power at just 8,000 rpm and would happily spin into the red in top, it appears that the gearing was far too low. If that were the case, it would obviously scorch away from the line like a bat out of hell. And since going up through the box at full chat took lightning fast reflexes to keep up with rapidly rising revs, I think the wrong gearing theory – probably a too small front sprocket – holds merit. But just how a brand-new bike came off the production line with the wrong gearing is a mystery which I can't explain.

And my third theory? Perhaps by some incredible coincidence it was a combination of both.

What do you think?

S. P. Muir